Construction Safety

Construction Safety

R.K. Mishra

Sr. Faculty and Safety Advisor
O&M Solutions P. Ltd., Bhubaneswar, Odisha
and
Formerly 'Chief of Safety' and
Chief Manager (Operation Technologies)
Tata Refractories Ltd., Belpahar, Odisha

AITBS PUBLISHERS, INDIA

J-5/6, Krishan Nagar, Delhi-110051 (INDIA)
Tel.: 22054798, 22549313
Fax: 011-22543416
Email: aitbs@bol.net.in & aitbsindia@gmail.com

First Edition : 2012

ISBN: 978-93-7473-494-0

Published by:
Virender Kumar Arya for
AITBS Publishers, India
J-5/6, Krishan Nagar, Delhi-110051 (INDIA)
Phone: 22054798, 22549313; Fax: 011-22543416
E-mail: aitbs@bol.net.in & aitbsindia@gmail.com

Printed by AITBS, Delhi

Preface

Safety is an inbuilt system in our body. Like safety, there are so many other good and bad systems are also inbuilt in our body. To remain safe we have to enhance our inbuilt safety system by regularly developing it and suppressing the bad system like 'daredevilnesses, from our work.

An attempt has been made to make all construction workers a safe construction worker. Construction industry is the core industry and for growth and prosperity these have to continue further and further. Huge quantity of money, material, manpower and machinery etc. are used in construction and all safe methods are being adopted for timely completion of the project. This will be possible only when there is no unwanted incident like accidents. To stop this menace from our projects we must develop safety culture right from day one of the construction. Safety is important, there is no second thought about this; but it should not be a lip service.

With this purpose in mind a step has been taken in this construction safety book. The materials have been collected from various sources, so that the first hand safety information may be available to the person interested.

–R.K. Mishra

Contents

CHAPTER 1

Construction Safety

NEED FOR SAFETY CULTURE IN CONSTRUCTION INDUSTRY

1. Some of the research findings related to construction industry by ILO are as below:
   - A study conducted in four industrialized countries – Canada, Japan, UK, and USA showed that the fatality rates in the construction industry were more than four times that of manufacturing.
   - More workers meet with accidents during the 1st year of their employment. In China, accident-prone age group is between 20-30.
   - There were more accidents caused by falling (working at height), persons being struck or trapped by objects in motion, scaffolds, electric shocks, construction machinery etc.
2. The possibility of labor accidents arising in the construction industry as opposed to all industries is over 40% and the percentage of fatalities is also

exceedingly high. Therefore, safety measures to be employed in the construction industry continue to be matters of urgent importance that must be further enforced.

3. Construction sites in developing countries are 10 times more dangerous than in industrialized nation and Indian sites are no exception.
4. An analysis of occupational accidents reveals that the accidents caused due to highly unsafe work conditions and actions account for 80% of all accidents.
5. In absence of "safety culture" in industry (unlike manufacturing sector) accident injuries and deaths always remained on the top (next to road accidents) at the national level.
6. In order to reduce potential occupational accidents and cut back occupational injuries, it is necessary that each workplace should adopt a management system for occupational safety and health, precisely identifying risk factors under this system and systematically and continuously develop the measures that should be taken to eliminate or reduce those risk factors.
7. It is important to continuously strive to reduce latent risk factors at workplaces as close to zero as possible.
8. Liberalization, privatization and globalization of Indian economy and consequent foreign investments in infra structural sector have changed the construction scenario dramatically. Multinationals have brought with them high standards of safety and health stipulations which Indian construction industry was not used to. In order to compete with these multinationals, it is essential that the Indian construction companies ensure that the safety management function is integrated with overall project management system

and safety culture is inculcated through, occupational safety health and environment management system.

9. It is necessary for the central government, employers, and workers and people in general to aggressively grapple with adherence to safety by them and strive to enhance the safety awareness of society as a whole.
10. It would be important to create safety culture as an issue common to the nation as a whole or, in other word, the organizations and individuals to foster their mindset in which safety takes top priority.

PREVENTING CONSTRUCTION ACCIDENTS

Major construction accidents at site were prevented by taking proactive actions such as

- Heavy equipment accidents were prevented by
  - developing operating procedures and their implementation
  - employing trained and skilled persons to operate
  - providing adequate signaling and supervision
  - providing overload preventing devices
  - installing warning devices such as back sensors, contact sensors, flashers equipped with warning buzzers
  - periodic preventive maintenance and upkeep.

Landslide accidents, collapse of natural ground were prevented by maintaining a safe excavation grade and height and by constructing protective shoring.

Falling accidents were prevented by making work floors and pathways as flat and slip proof as possible and building handrails, fences in the work area, obstructing openings with scaffolding safety nets, safety ropes etc.

Providing nets, sheeting, reinforcement using bracing cable or other means prevented collapses of scaffolding/ structures.

Accidents caused by falling objects during construction work were prevented by construction plan that avoids work being performed in both high and low work areas at the same time, by using netting, construction sheeting, mesh sheeting, by binding materials together when placing them in high work areas, by building a drop chute and prohibiting access to hazardous area.

All workers were given appropriate personal protective equipments (PPE) while performing their jobs in order to protect their body parts from variety of hazards. Strict enforcement to use PPE (by both men and women) and maintenance of PPE resulted in significant reduction in minor injuries as well as reduction in number of first aid services.

SAFETY IN CONSTRUCTION INDUSTRY

1. Introduction

The construction industry is one of the oldest and most hazardous industries contributing to a high rate of fatalities and serious accidents. Statutory protection has now been provided through **Construction Safety Act** or otherwise known as **"Building and other Construction Workers (Regulation of Employment and Conditions of Services) Act, 1996.**

2. Objectives

The Act has been made to provide Safety, Health and Welfare measures and give construction workers a **Social Security.**

3. Responsibility of the Employer

The law requires that the employer should provide:

- A safe practice for work
- A safe system for work
- Safe access to and from the place of work
- Safe plant and equipment.

4. Duties and Responsibilities of Workers

- Report the defects in the lifting device/gears without unreasonable delay.
- No building worker, shall unless duly authorized, remove or interfere with any fencing, gangway, gear, ladder, life saving appliances, covering, lighting or other things whatsoever required by the Act. If any aforesaid things are removed, the persons engaged in the work shall restore such things at the end of the period, during which its removal was necessary.
- Every building worker shall use only means of access provided in accordance with the rules.
- It shall be the duty of a building worker to keep the latrines, urinals, washing points, canteen and other facilities provided by the employer, for securing his welfare, in a clean and hygienic condition.

ACCIDENT PREVENTION (MANAGEMENT ASPECTS)

1. **Safety Manual:** Prepare a safety manual for the company.
2. **Safety Co-ordinator:** Depute full time/part time safety coordinators depending upon the size of the project site and nature of hazards.
3. **Worker Screening:** Screening of workmen.
4. **Project Safety Plan:** Prepare a Project Safety Plan and implement at job sites which covers:

    (a) *Overall scope of work:* Fabrication, erection, excavation, concreting, brickwork, finishing work, painting, blasting, non distructive tests, etc.

(b) *Obligation chart:* Responsibility of the line functionaries and reporting of the safety engineering functions.

(c) *Safety committee (all jobsites):*

- Structure: Chairman, Secretary and Members
- Roles and responsibilities
- Project Manager
- Safety committee members
- Safety coordinators
- Site engineers
- First line supervisors/Engineers
- Subcontractors.

(d) *Job related specific PPE*

(e) *General site safety rules:*

- Use of PPE and safety devices relevant to site activities.
- General house keeping, stacking of materials.
- Road safety inside the projects.
- Access/egress and workstation safety.
- Safe use of construction power.
- Work permit system:
  - Hot work permit
  - Excavation clearance permit
  - Industrial radiography permit
  - Permit to work on overhead traction line
  - Permit to work on plant and machinery and other power driven equipment
  - Electrical work permit (HT and LT)
  - Permit to open manhole covers/grills
  - Permit for confined space entry.

(f) Use, maintenance and inspection of plant and machinery.

(g) Scaffolding norms.

(h) Use of safe materials handling and personal handling equipment.

(i) Fire prevention and protection.

(j) Contingency plan.

(k) Others.

5. Identification of High Risk/Hazardous Operations in the Site and their Appropriate Safety Measures:

(a) Structural and equipment erection.

(b) Excavation.

(c) Concreting – Chimney, silos, cooling towers etc.

(d) Pre-casting and pre-cast erection.

(e) Pile driving.

(f) Road works: existing roads/new roads.

(g) Work over water.

(h) Blasting.

(i) Use, handling, storage of compressed gas cylinders etc.

(j) Pressure testing – hydraulic and pneumatic.

(k) Tunneling.

(l) Others.

6. Peptalk.

7. Checklists and Reports

General site safety inspections: Excavation, demolition, blasting, scaffoldings, ladders, working platforms, PPE, structural fabrication and erection, gas cutting and welding, means of access, electrical work, house keeping, fire prevention and protection, road safety, first aid box, illumination, safety boards, posters, stickers, drinking water, sanitation, emergency vehicles.

- Electrical safety inspection
- Erection safety inspection
- Scaffolding inspection
- Safety while working at height
- Cranes inspection
- Vehicle and earth moving equipment inspection.

8. **Statistics and Reports**
9. **Accident Investigation Report**
   (a) Action taken report
   (b) Weekly analysis of accidents
   (c) Monthly safety statistics
   (d) Register of first aid
   (e) Subcontractors' safety performance evaluation.
10. **Job Safety Analysis**

Identity of task: Asbestos roof sheeting at 25 meters height.

Sl. No.	Sequence of operation activity steps	Hazards involved at various steps	Safety measures/ precautions	Responsiblity/ action by
1.	Reaching to 25 mtrs. height	Slip and fall from height	Approach ladder/staircase to be provided	Execution engineer
2.	Walking on trusses and purlins	Fall from height	– safety nets, below – lifeline – mobile type fall arrestors	Execution engineer

			– safety belts – Crawling boards after providing the asbestos sheets – safety helmets – Close supervision	

Date:

Signature: ____________________

Executive Engineer Safety Coordinator

11. Third Party (competent person) Inspection, examination and testing of:

- Hoists and Lifts (Sec. – 28), once in six months.
- Lifting machines (crane, crab, winch, pulley block etc.) and lifting tackles (chain, rope sling, hook, D-shackle, coupling, spider or similar appliances – (Sec. 29), once in 12 months.

12. Safety Training

13. Safety Awareness Programme.

SAFETY MEASURES WHILE COMMISIONING PROJECTS

The rate of industrial accidents in India is almost double than that of U.K. and three times that of U.S.A. per thousand workers. The basic reason for this cause is that we have to depend much more on man power rather than on mechanical means. The man power is comparatively cheap and readily available in India.

The most affected categories of employees are the contractor's labors that are ignorant about the hidden hazards at work sites and the contractor who adopts the philosophy of work execution at minimum cost. This work force is usually of temporary nature and as frequently changes their jobs. They are not well versed about safety aspects of the job. It is very essential for the entire workman including contractor's labor to use proper recommended personal protective equipment like:

1. Safety helmets.
2. Face shields.
3. Noise protection equipment like ear muff, ear plugs etc.
4. Rubber, canvas leather and PVC type of hand gloves.
5. Safety shoes.
6. Nose masks/dust masks.
7. Rubber, cotton, PVC type apron clothing.

Contractor's establishments, because of their continuous violation of safety rules, continuous vigil should be done against them.

The rate of accidents occurring during construction/execution phase is much more than when the plants are in running stage. The hazards during construction/erection are grouped as under:

1. Deep excavations.
2. Working on heights.
3. Electrical installations.
4. Mobile cranes and tools/tackles engaged in structural equipment/erection activities.
5. Heavy vehicles plying on kuchha roads.
6. Design aspects have not been taken care of safety requirement.

Right from the beginning of civil work, safety aspects at site to be given prime importance.

1. Daily site visit and spot action.
2. Weekly site surveys and review.
3. Site safety committee meetings.
4. Inspection of lifting machines.
5. Inspection of fire fighting system.
6. Accident reporting and investigation.
7. Workshop on safety.
8. Safety awareness.

Zero accident is the aim in our project commissioning and try to achieve this.

Safety in Vehicular Movement

(Hazard identification and preventive measures at project site)

Hazard	Consequences	Preventive measures
Reversing the vehicle	• Hurt people • Severe injuries • Fatal	• Ensure to drive the vehicle by competent driver • Provide reverse horn on the vehicle level

Safety in Piling Work

(Hazard identification and preventive measures at project site)

Hazard	Consequences	Preventive measures
Failure of pile driving equipment	Hurt people	Inspect piling rigs and pulley blocks before the beginning of each shift.
Noise pollution	Deafness and Psychological imbalance	Use PPE, i.e., ear plug, ear muff.

Extruding rods/casing	Hurt people	• Barricade the area • Install sign boards • Provide first aid
Working in the vicinity of live-electricity	Electrocution/ Asphyxiation	• Shutoff the supply • Keep safe distance from live electricity • Provide artificial/rescue breathing to the injured.

Safety in Narrow Deep Excavation for Pipelines

(Hazard identification and preventive measures at project site)

Hazard	Consequences	Preventive measures
Frequent in or slides	• Severe injuries/Fatal case • Damage to adjoining structure	• Barricade the excavated area • Maintain at least two meter distance from edge of cut • Strengthen shoring • Provide escape ladder
Flooding due to hydro testing	Drowning situation	• Pump out accumulated water • Maintain adequate ventilation

Safety in Rock Excavation by Blasting

(Hazard identification and preventive measures at project site)

Hazard	Consequences	Preventive measures
Explosion	• Severe injuries/Fatal • Damage to adjoining structure	• Barricade the blasting area • Allow authorized person to perform blasting operation • Smoking and open flames are to be strictly prohibited • Contain the explosion intensity by sand bags, old tyres

Scattering of stone pieces entrapping of persons/ animals	• Hurt people • Severe injuries • Fatal	• Barricade the area with red flag • Blow siren before blasting • Use PPE, i.e., Helmet, Goggles, and face cover
Misfire	Sudden explosion	• Do not return to site unless announced safe by competent person

Safety in Excavation for Digging Pit

(Hazard identification and preventive measures at project site)

Hazard	Consequences	Preventive measures
Fall into pit	Serious injury	• Provide barricade with warning signal • Provide sufficient lights • Provide two entries/exit • Provide emergency ladder
Earth collapse	• Suffocation/ Breathlessness • Buried Death	• Keep soil away from the edge • Provide suitable size of shoring • Keep soil out from the edge • Don't allow vehicle to operate too close to the excavated areas • Maintain sufficient angle of repose • Provide bench of 0.5 Mt. depth of excavation except hard rock soil.
Contact with buried electric cables, Gas/oil Pipelines	Electrocution explosion	• Obtain work permit before digging • Locate the position of buried utilities by referring drawings • Start digging manually to locate the exact position of buried of utilities

Flooding due to excessive underground water	Drowning situation	• Provide suitable size of dewatering pump • Provide ring buoys
Digging in the vicinity of existing building	• Collapse of building/ structure • Loss of life and property	• Obtain prior approval • Construct retaining wall side by side
Movement of vehicles/ equipment close to the edge of cut	• Slides or cave-in • Buried	• Barricade the excavated area • Maintain at least two meter distance from edge of cut • Strengthen shoring

SAFETY IN EXCAVATION AND FOUNDATION

Construction activities are associated with safety and health risks at worksites because of their magnitude and complex nature. Construction job involves multitude of civil work activities. Nearly 30% of cost of erection is expended in civil construction like offices, warehouses, township etc. Contractors, engaging contract labors execute all such works. The safety of the contract labor during excavation is main concern of this topic.

The accident rate in construction is 4 to 5 times higher than that of manufacturing sector. The analysis of accidents by causes shows that

- 84% of the injured employees are below 30 yrs. of the age.
- 83% accident occurred to unskilled and semiskilled labors.
- Work at height is the most hazardous factor.
- Rainy season, wet season and highest temperature.

- Overhead operations in scaffolds tower cranes and temporary holes etc.

Major Causes of Accidents are

- falling from height
- machine tools and hand tools
- burns
- electricity
- explosion and fire
- hit by moving objects
- lifting machines
- material handling
- road accidents.

Keeping in view of the above causes construction activities need to give more attention on the following civil activities to provide minimum safety requirements to the contract labors.

Safety in Excavation

- Loose material to be stored near edges distance from edge = depth of 1500 mm whichever is more.
- Falling objects around the site of excavation.
- Barricading with railing of the areas.
- Adequate illumination.
- Placing of warning signals around excavation site.
- Bracing of side of excavation.
- Benching of slopes.
- Sheeting of excavated area.
- Provision of ladders for deep trenches.
- Safety appliances for workman.
- Provision for dewatering.
- Undercutting.

- Two approaches and their slopes railing etc.
- Wet soil condition, water seepage.
- Underground pipelines, cables etc.
- Earliest concerting.

Concreting of Foundation

- Ensure that the faces of eastern walls all around properly stored and restricted to avoid earth sliding.
- Safe approach to be provided for concrete mixer carriers to approach the area.
- A person should be available to guide the vehicle while reversing the same in work area.
- The driving mechanism of concrete mixer should be well guarded.
- Hydraulic system of the pump, electrical cables of drive should be well guarded.
- The concreting vibrator hoses should be mechanically locked.
- Tested lifting tools and tackles should be used.
- Shuttering should be well supported from all sides.
- Platform provided should be at least 1 m wide railing and toe board.

SAFETY PROCEDURE FOR WORKING AT HEIGHT BY COTRACTOR'S WORKERS

REQUIREMENT OF WORKERS FOR WORKING AT HEIGHT

1. Every worker to be deployed for working at height shall be examined and certified by a Registered Medical Practitioner for physical and medical fitness and freedom from epilepsy, high blood pressure, obesity and vertigo.

2. Every worker before deployment for working at height shall be imparted the training for working at height which shall include the competency in the use of safety belts and allied equipment. This training shall be in addition to the general safety training imparted by the safety-engineering department.
3. After successful completion of training and tests, the workers shall be issued a height pass, which shall be valid for a maximum period of one year. On expiry it shall be renewed after the worker passes the test once again.

Execution of Work at Height

1. Contractors shall make height work procedure applicable for compliance whenever they deploy workers.
2. **Height pass:** A document to be issued to a worker for working at height after imparting him the necessary training as per the specimen given at **Appendix A.**
3. **Safety requirements/precautions:** Before starting a work at height, all the safety requirements (like safety belts, protective helmets and safety nets) shall be decided as per the need of the area/ site by the executing agency in collaboration with the safety officer and the contractor. These shall be documented; a suggested checklist is given at **Appendix B.**
4. Safety net shall be used whenever considered necessary by the executing officer and the safety officer. Safety net made of non-flammable material shall be used where there is a possibility of welding spark, molten material, burning spark of material, etc., falling on it.
5. Before starting the day's work, the site shall be inspected by the executing officer for ensuring

compliance of all safety aspects. After ensuring compliance of all safety aspects, the contractor, the executing officer and the safety officer shall sign the document given at Appendix B giving clearance for starting the work. In the event of discontinuation of the work and before re-starting, the site inspection shall be redone, as above by the execution officer.

6. Supervision by supervisors or executives shall be ensured for 100% of the time.
7. Work at height shall be permitted only when a reasonable level of sun-light is available as per the discretion of the contractor, the Executing Officer and the Safety Officer. The work shall not be permitted in cloudy weather because of the possibility of electrocution by lightening or even getting started by the sound of thunder and thereby falling down. When work at height is done indoors, there shall be adequate illumination.

Appendix A

SPECIMEN OF HEIGHT PASS

______________ Plant

Safety Engineering Department

Photo of worker with seal of issuing authority

Height Pass No. ______________

This is to certify that the under mentioned person has been permitted to work at height.

Name:______________________________

Father's Name:______________________________

Designation:______________________________

Age:________________________

Validity Up to:________________________

Signature/Left
thumb Impression of worker:________________________

Signature of Authorized
Executive of Safety Engg. Dept.:________________________

Name & Seal:________________________

Appendix B

CHECKLIST OF REQUIREMENTS/ PRECAUTIONS FOR WORKING AT HEIGHT

1. Name of the department executing the job.
2. Name of the department representative(s).
3. Name(s) of contractor's supervisors.
4. Name of contractor.
5. Exact location of work.
6. Brief description of work.
7. No. of person deployed for the job.
8. Names of the persons deployed to do the job at height.
9. No. of persons issued height passes.
10. Reference no. of height passes issued.
11. All persons have been imparted training for working at height by safety engineering Department . Yes/No
12. Head of operation department has been informed of this job. Yes/No
13. Shut down of following operating equipments have been obtained

    EOT cranes Yes/No

    Belt conveyors Yes/No

Gas lines Yes/No

Bus bars Yes/No

14. Checking of scaffoldings/ladders done and found O.K. Yes/No
15. Supply of safety belt ensured. Yes/No
16. Supply of protective helmets ensured. Yes/No
17. Provision of safety nets for arresting fall of personnel. Made/Not Reqd.
18. Weather is clear to do the job (outdoor job). Yes/No
19. Illumination is adequate to do the job (indoor work). Yes/No
20. Satisfactory house keeping conditions (sharp objects, redundant cables, and structural, slippery objects like oils and lubricants do not exist and shall not be allowed in the working area). Yes/No
21. Special remarks on (a) period of validity (b) the quality of P.P.E's.

Inspected the site and permitted to start the work.

Name, Designation, Signature and Date of

1. The Contractor
2. Executing Officer
3. Safety Officer.

Safety While Working at Height

(Hazard identification and preventive measures at project site)

Hazard	Consequences	Preventive measures
Fall down	➢ Severe injury ➢ Fatal	➢ Obtain work permit after medical fitness certificate ➢ Provide barricade/guard rails at the work place

		➢ Provide proper working space, i.e., at least .6 m × .6 m ➢ Tie/weld working platform with fixed structure ➢ Provide lifeline on the beam and install fall arrest system, i.e., safety net etc. ➢ Use PPE like full body harness safety helmet, safety shoe etc.
Material can fall down	➢ Severe injury ➢ Fatal	➢ Keep the workplace neat and clean ➢ Remove the scrap immedia-tely ➢ Barricade the area at ground level ➢ Don't throw/ drop materials or equipments from height ➢ Remove scrap from planks ➢ All tools to be carried in a tool kit bag ➢ Ensure wearing of helmet by the employees at low level.

THE DON'TS FOR THE WORKING AT HEIGHT

1. No loose dress like Dhoti/Lungi are allowed;
2. Work without hot permit never to be encouraged;
3. The people other than with adequate experience and having attention to safety measures need not be deployed for working at height;
4. Before the worker reaches the height, never allow him to do the work without checking his physical standards like blood pressure etc. on daily basis;
5. Ensure working of safety measures and safety belts on daily basis before work commences;
6. Avoid using sleepers or loose foot-wear;

7. No mechanical load would be carried by human being individually, i.e., work should not commence without ensuring material supply (like asbestos/corrugated sheets for replacement etc.) by Joists/Lifts/Cranes etc.;
8. No supervisor or managerial personnel should instruct to carryout maintenance, construction, overhaul regarding work at a height without the issuance/ experience of safety work permit for the same.

Specific training programs need to be designed for carrying out the work at height considering different required factors.

Hazards Associated and Individual Requirement for Working at Height

1. **Type of Activity/Job**

   Working at Height
2. **Hazard/Risk involved**

   Giddiness, Vertigo, Falling down resulting in injury, Slipping of tools, Sparks, fall from openings etc.
3. **Damaging Source of Energy**

   Kinetic Energy
4. **Remedial Measures**

   Training, Height Pass, Safety Belt, Strong platform with toe boards.

The major basic requirement of Individual stamina for their suitability for working at height

1. Sound health;
2. Consistent normal blood pressure;
3. Devoid of long illness, epilepsy, giddiness;
4. Mentally balanced and sound;
5. Always attentive in work;
6. Issuance of hot work permit for that area where the job is carrying out at height;

7. Ensuring fastening of safety belts with the nearby strong support/struss members;
8. Proper selection of tools for specific working (along with definite safety measures, say the hammer or the toolbit need to be attached to the belt of the worker so that any slippage of this may not allow it to fall from great height straight to the ground level);
9. Placement of Guard Rails;
10. Proper lifting devices should be used to place the persons on the desired spot at height where the work will be carried on otherwise the men will be exhausted and loosing their physical stamina before the work commences.

Wherever any work is carried out at height first thing is to ensure safe system of work. The next important thing is the role of Line Managers/Supervisors to ensure safety.

Scaffolding in England: More Than 'Just A Job'

In England, scaffold building is considered a craft, on the same level as heating and air conditioning, brick masonry, electrical work and other specialized construction functions. Unlike the United States, where training is left largely to the private sector, a British government agency, the construction industry training board, provides training for all levels of scaffolders.

A requirement for regularly, scheduled inspections is one of the principal differences between scaffold – safety regulation in the United States and England.

While OSHA also requires regular inspections, British law mandates that a "competent person" performs them at least once a week and record them in a book prescribed for the purpose. "Any fault found must be put right before the scaffold is used again," according to the British Health and Safety Executive.

While British standard 5973 provides a detailed "code of practice" for scaffolds, basic safety requirements are spelled out in nontechnical language in two documents, each two pages, available from the HSE. One pertains to general-access scaffolds, the other to prefabricated aluminum tower scaffolds. Both provide commonsense guidelines. For example:

Brick guards or other means of vertical protection, such as netting, should be provided where there is a risk of materials falling. Where this risk is very high, for example during demolition of façade cleaning, additional protection in the form of scaffold fans should also be provided. Never throw materials from the scaffold. Where possible, use mechanical hoists or rubbish chutes to dispose of the material.

Only competent scaffolders should erect and dismantle scaffolds. Never remove ties to gain access for work. When dismantling the scaffolds, the scaffolder should ensure that sufficient ties are in place. The ties should not be removed until the scaffold has been dismantled down to the level.

All scaffolds require bracing (the provisions of diagonal tubes to introduce strength via triangulation) to prevent them from collapsing. Sufficient façade (sway) and ledger bracing should be provided to sustain the structural stability of the scaffold. The standard should be plumb and must always be supported on steel base plates. Brick and other loose material are quite unsuitable for this purpose and should never be used. If the ground is soft, it should be well leveled and compacted and timber sole plates used to spread the load.

When towers are used in public places, additional precautions may be necessary. Barriers should be erected at ground level to prevent people from walking into the tower or work area. If it is so remain in position unattended, the access ladders should be removed or boarded over to prevent unauthorized access. If used on a pavement… a license may be required from the local authority.

Use of Ladders

Placement workmen should observe the following practices when placing ladders:

1. Place a ladder so that the horizontal distance from the base to the vertical plane of the support is approximately one-fourth the ladder length between the supports. (For example, place a 12-foot ladder so that the bottom is 3 feet away from the object against which the top is leaning.)
2. Do not use ladders in a horizontal position as runways or as scaffolds. Single and extension ladders are designed for use in a nearly vertical position with the base removed from the wall, and can not be safely used in a horizontal position with the base removed from the wall, and can not be safely used in a horizontal position or with the base at a greater distance from the wall than that indicated above.
3. Never place a ladder against a windowpane or sash. Securely fasten a board (not with nails) across the top of the ladders to give a bearing at each side of the window. On wide windows with metal sash, the bearing may be across the mullions or between window jambs.
4. Never place a ladder in front of a door, which opens toward the ladder unless the door is locked, blocked or otherwise guarded.
5. Place portable ladders so that the both side rails have secure footing. Provide solid footing on soft ground to prevent the ladder from sinking.
6. Be sure that ladder feet are not placed on movable objects, but on a substantial and level base.
7. Never lean a ladder against loose boxes, barrels, round objects or other unsafe backing.

8. When you use a ladder for access to high place, securely lash or otherwise fasten the ladder to prevent its slipping.
9. Secure both bottom and top to prevent displacement when using a ladder for access to a scaffold, and extend the ladder side rails at least 3½ feet above the top landing.

Types of Ladders

Single ladders over 30 feet in length should not be used. Portable single ladders should be built with spread side rails, with the width between the side rails at the base not less than 11½ inches for ladders up to and including 10 feet in length. For longer ladders, this width should be increased at least 1/4 inch for each additional foot of length.

Extension ladders: Two-section extension ladders should be no longer than 60 feet.

Stepladders: Should never be more than 20 feet long. Stepladders are manufactured in three groups as follows.

- Type I – 4 to 20 feet (heavy duty)
- Type II – 4 to 12 feet (medium duty)
- Type III – 3 to 8 feet (light duty)

Trolley and side-rolling ladders: Should be no more than 20 feet long. The width between side rails should be at least 12 inches, with the minimum dimension for side rails 25/32 inch by 3 inches for ladders up to and including 10 feet, and 25/32 inch by 3¼ inches for ladders over 10 and up to and including 20 feet, when constructed of spruce or equivalent.

Trestle ladders and extension or base sections of extension trestle ladders should be no more than 20 feet long.

Fixed ladders should be installed in a preferred pitch range between 75 and 90 degrees with the horizontal. The distance between the centerline of rungs, cleats, or steps and the nearest permanent object in back of the ladder should be not less than 7 inches. The distance between rungs or cleats should not exceed 12 inches or should be uniform throughout the length of the ladder. Rungs should have a minimum diameter of 3/4 inch.

Fixed ladders should have parallel sides of either wood or metal and should be permanently fastened at top, bottom, and intermediate locations. A fixed ladder 20 feet and more in length should be provided with a cage or basket guard.

Fixed ladders over 30 feet long should be built in zigzag sections and, unless cages are used, should be provided with safety platforms at intervals of not more than 20 feet. Rungs should be omitted above the working or landing platform, and the side rails should be carried 3½ feet higher and preferably goosenecked. Openings more than 18 inches wide between the ladder and the working platform should be provided by a landing platform. Where the step-across distance from the center line of the rung of the ladder to the nearest edge of structure or equipment is more than 12 inches, a landing platform should be provided. Several types of equipment have been devised for use with fixed ladders to protect workman from falls.

Roof ladders should be constructed with either metal or wood side rails or rungs, and should be made to conform to the specifications for fixed ladders.

Landing platforms should be equipped with standard railings and toe boards and so arranged as to give safe access to the ladder. Platforms should be not less than 24 inches wide.

Fire ladders: Many aluminum fire ladders are being used, as well as wood ladders. Fire ladders should be light but strong, marked for **fire purposes only**, and stored so that they can be obtained easily and quickly in an emergency. Aluminum fire ladders should be marked with a warning that they are not to be used near electrical equipment.

A single cleat ladder longer than 30 feet should not be used.

A double cleat ladder longer than 24 feet should not be used.

Ladder Safety

- Use portable ladders safely to prevent falls.
- Falls are most common accident with ladders.
- The man climbing on the ladder should be straight.
- Avoid an unstable support for climbing on ladders.
- Use well designed wooden ladders.
- Avoid using metallic ladders as they are good conductors of electricity.
- To prevent skidding, place ladders on a firm ground.
- The slope of ladders should be one out of every four up.
- Do not use a ladder under the influence of drugs/ alcohol.
- Avoid jumping from a ladder.
- Provide warning signs to prevent someone walking under the ladder.
- Ensure adequate hand hold in ladders.
- Avoid standing on the top two rungs of the ladder.
- Inspect ladders regularly for defects.
- Avoid using ladders having missing rungs.
- Keep defective ladders out of service.
- Painting a ladder may hide the cracks.

- Keep the ladders in its right place after the use.

Ladder Inspection Check List

Type of ladder	Item to be checked	Condition O.K.	Repair needs
General	• Loose steps or rungs • Loose nails, screws, bolts, or other metal parts • Cracked, split, or broken uprights, braces, steps or rungs • Silver on uprights, rungs or steps • Damaged or worn nonslip bases.		
Stepladders	• Wobbly (from side strain) • Defective locks that do not seat properly when the ladder is extended • Deterioration of rope, from exposure to acid or either destructive agents.		
Trolley ladders	• Worn or missing tires • Wheels that bind • Floor wheel brackets broken or loose • Floor wheels and brackets missing • Ladders binding in guides • Ladder and rail stops broken, loose or missing • Rail supports broken or section of rail missing • Trolley wheels out of adjustment.		

Trestle ladders	• Loose in hinges • Wobbly • Loose or bent hinge spreaders • Stop broken on hinge spreader • Center section guide for extension out of alignment • Defective locks for extension.		
Sectional ladders	• Worn or loose metal parts • Wobbly.		
Fixed ladders	• Loose, worn, or damaged rungs or side rails • Damaged or corroded parts of cage • Corroded bolts or revet heads on inside of metal stacks • Damaged or corroded handrails or brackets on platforms • Weakened or damaged rungs on brick or concrete slabs • Base of ladder obstructed.		
Fire Ladders	• Marking illegible • Improperly stored • Storage obstructed.		

Safe Practices while Using Ladders

Workmen should observe these safe practices when using ladders:

1. Do not use makeshift ladders, such as cleats fastened across a single rail.

2. Be sure that a stepladder is fully open before you use it.
3. Before using a ladder, inspect it for defects. Never use a defective ladder.
4. Tag or mark a defective ladder so that it will be repaired or destroyed.
5. Do not splice short ladders together. They are designed for use in their original lengths, and are not strong enough for use in greater lengths. Also, most splicing methods, particularly "on the job methods", are not safe.
6. Keep ladders clean and free from dirt and grease which might conceal defects.
7. Do not use ladders during a strong wind except in emergency, and then only when they are securely tied.
8. Do not leave ladders unattended, especially outdoors, unless they are anchored at top and bottom.

Learn to Lift Safely

1. Think before you do any thing.
2. Stand as close to the load as you can, and spread your feet to form a stable base. If the object to be lifted is on a shelf or racking, slide the load close to you.
3. Bend your knees, keeping your back in a natural line. Don't bend right down, though: if you bend your knees too much if it will reduce your power to lift.
4. Grasp the load firmly with your hands, not just your fingers. If the load is rough or awkwardly shaped, remember to be wearing protective gloves.
5. Raise your head up as you start to lift.
6. Lift using your legs, not your back. Move your feet.
7. Hold the loads close to the center of your body as you move.

8. Make sure that you can see where you are going.
9. Don't twist your body: this is a major cause of injury.
10. And finally, remember that when you lift your back is supporting you and the load. Always follow the ten-point guide and you should avoid injury.

Alternative Lift: Carrying the Load

- Do keep the load close to your body as you move.
- Do keep your arms tucked in: this avoids putting extra strain on your shoulder and neck muscles.
- Do face the place where you are going to put down your load by turning both your feet and body in the right direction.
- Do make sure that your field of vision is clear when carrying a load. If the object you are carrying is too big to see over, then get help from a workmate or use a mechanical aid.
- Do not release or change your grip on the load unless the weight is otherwise supported. You could drop your load.
- Do not stoop, twist your body, or lean back. Move your feet if you have to change direction while carrying your load.

...And Unloading

- Bend your knees
- Mind your body
- Ease the load
- Place the load
- And once the load is in place make sure it is secure before you walk away from it.

LIFTING MACHINES

There are different types of lifting machines, such as EOT cranes, HOT crane, Jib crane, Chain Pulley Blocks, Hoists etc. These are required to be used carefully to ensure safety of men and material.

Do's

1. Check the equipment and connected accessories at the beginning of each shift.
2. Know the capacity of the lifting machines.
3. Secure the load properly and firmly.
4. Raise the load slowly.
5. Avoid sudden stopping or reversals, except in emergencies.
6. Ensure long travel and cross travel brakes are working.
7. Ensure limit switches are working.
8. Ensure power-indication lamps are working.
9. Follow the signals while carrying the load.
10. Ensure that all switches in the pendant box of the pendant operated crane are in good condition.
11. Lift the load only to the required height.
12. Ensure hook latches are in place while handling the load.

Don'ts

1. Do not carry the load without properly balancing it.
2. Do not carry load over persons and machines.
3. Do not allow the load to remain suspended.
4. Do not overload equipment beyond the capacity.
5. Do not allow more than one person to give signals.
6. Do not use the equipment for pulling the load.
7. Do not create jerk while transferring the load.
8. Do not ride on the load.

Safety in Handling and Lifting Equipment

(Hazard identification and preventive measures at project site)

Hazard	Consequences	Preventive measures
Failure of load lifting and moving equipments	• Hurt people • Severe injuries/fatal • Property damage	• Check periodically oil brakes, gears, horns and tyre pressure of all moving machinery • Check quality size and condition of all chain pulley blocks, slings, U-clamps, D-shackles, wire ropes etc. • Allow lifting slings as short as possible • Allow crane to move only on hard, firm and leveled ground.
Overload of lifting equipment	• Hurt people • Severe injuries/fatal • Property damage	• Safe lifting capacity of derricks and winches should be ascertained before lifting • Safe working load shall be marked on all lifting equipment • Check the weight of the lifting items. Paint the weight of the lifting items • Decide the angle of erection before lifting • Allow only trained operators and riggers during crane operations
Overhead electrical	• Electrocution • Fire	➢ Do not allow boom or other parts of crane to come within 3 m wires reach of overhead HT cables.

Safety Harness and Lanyard

Why do I have to wear a safety harness and lanyard?

- To arrest a fall from height.

- Because it has been provided by your employer-for your safety.
- Because you have a legal obligation to wear it. The Health and Safety Executive can prosecute you.

Do I need to check my harness and lanyard before use?

Your lanyard and harness need to be checked and inspected regularly. Things to be checked include:

- Knots in lanyard other than those provided by the manufacturer.
- Surface abrasion across the face of webbing and at webbing loops.
- Abrasion at the edges of webbing.
- Cuts to webbing, rope or stitching, particularly at the edges (e.g., where the lanyard may have been choke hitched around steel work, this practice is not recommended).
- Areas that have been subjected to chemical attack, which can result in weakening and softening-often indicated by flaking of the surface. There may also be a change to the color of the fibers.
- Heat of friction damage indicated by fibers with a glazed appearance, which may feel harder than surrounding fibers.
- Damaged or deformed fittings (e.g., carabineers, screw link connectors, scaffold hooks).
- Ultra-violet degradation which is difficult to identify, particularly visually, but there may be some loss of color (if dyed) and a powdery surface.
- Partially deployed energy absorber (e.g., short pull out of tear webbing).
- Contamination (e.g., with dirt, grit, sand, etc.) which may result in internal or external abrasion.

Limitation of Safety Belt:

- Harness should be the personal property of the user.
- The strength of the anchor device should be greater than 10 KN and the anchor point be situated above user's head.
- It should not be used in highly acid or basic environment.

Checklist at the Time of Purchase:

- Confirming to the ISI standard.
- Identification of the manufacturer.
- Type of product code.
- Batch No./Lot No.
- Year of manufacture.
- Material.
- Size.

Tips for Structural Painting

Falls from height often have serious consequences, and may even result in death or permanent, partial or total disability. Hence ropes, safety lines, belt and fall arrester should be provided and used.

Improvised and inadequate make shift arrangements should not be used in the place of the ladder, work platform etc.

Defective scaffolding can be the cause of serious accidents. Hence scaffolding should be in safe condition.

The habit of climbing on to machinery, equipment or to fittings in order to reach something, or of using cranes, stools, chairs, tables, fitments, sacks and barrels instead of correct and safe means of access, is a bad although widespread one which is the cause of many accidents.

Leaning out sideways whilst on a ladder and work platform is a dangerous habit. As soon as the body's center of gravity lies beyond the line of the stiles, the ladder is in unstable equilibrium and may topple over. In most cases, it will not be possible to avoid a fall.

Personal protective equipments such as gloves, masks, safety belts must be used.

At the end of the shift, the employees should wash his body thoroughly to prevent occupational disease.

Safety in Radiography

(Hazard identification and preventive measures at project site)

Hazard	Consequences	Preventive measures
Ionization/ radiation from source	• Cancer • Dermatitis • Skin irritation	• Follow safety guidelines before commencement of the job • Employ authorized and trained persons • Barricade the area and install Radiation warning symbol • Prohibit unauthorized entries • Wear requisite PPE and film badges issued.
Transpor-tation and storage of Radiography source	• Cancer • Dermatitis • Skin irritation	• Never touch or handle radiography source with hands • Store radiography source inside approved pit in an exclusive isolated storage room with lock and key arrangements • Radiography source should not be carried either in passenger bus or in a passenger compartment of the train • Inform authority before source movement.

Loss of Radioisotope	• Cancer • Dermatitis • Skin irritation	• Try to locate with the help of survey meter • Inform the authority.

Approach by Construction Industries in Japan

Safety Cycle – The most powerful technique

1. **Morning safety ritual (daily everyone participating):** Every morning prior to work, all workers at site gather together and after physical exercises, a few words are spoken by the site manager conveying the results of the previous day's inspection at the end of the day together with the orders of the day, pointers concerning safety measures for the day together with detailed directions deemed necessary for the day.
2. **Safety meeting:** Every morning before commencing work and right after the morning ritual, everyone is discussed to convene in-groups according to skills (scaffolding workers, carpenters for concrete molds, electrician's etc.) and the site manager indicates the tasks for the day, the special precautions concerning safety etc., are given orally to the respective workers concerned. Following which everyone speaks about foreseeable danger zones and precautions considered necessary for the day's work.
3. **Inspection prior to start of work:** Prior to starting work, the tools and machinery to be used for the day are inspected together with an inspection of the site.
4. **Inspection rounds of the site manager:** The Site Manager shall conduct inspection rounds checking conditions and in his spot-checking, shall give appropriate directions concerning safety precautions.
5. **Directing and overseeing work in progress:** While work is progressing, the persons responsible for safety and health, the site manager and the site monitor shall

direct and oversee the work of the staff and eliminate unsafe working conditions and also unsafe action taken by workers, etc.

5. **Discuss safety procedures:** The main contractors and subcontractors (specialized skills) shall convene to discuss scheduling the following day's work (methods to be employed), the order of work together with safety measures to be employed.
6. **Cleaning up each area of responsibility:** All of the workers involved shall together before closing, clean up and put the whole site in order.
7. **Checking site at close of work:** At the end of work, the safety monitor of the main contractor and the site managers of the specialist groups, etc. shall conduct checks on site for steps taken concerning prevention of fire, theft, third party injury, damage or accidents.

❑ ❑ ❑

CHAPTER 2

Construction Site Safety

SAFE PLACES OF WORK IN PROJECTS

- Can everyone on the project reach their place of work safely, e.g., are roads, gangways, passageways, passenger hoists, staircases, ladders and scaffolds in good condition?
- Are there guard rails or equivalent protection to stop falls from open edges on scaffolds, mobile elevating work platforms, buildings, gangways, excavations, etc.?
- Are all holes and openings securely guard railed, provided with an equivalent standard of edge protection or provided with fixed, clearly marked covers to prevent falls?
- Are the working structures stable, adequately braced and not overloaded?
- Are all working areas and walkways level and free from trip hazards, obstructions such as stored material and waste?

- Is our site tidy, and are materials stored safely?
- Have we arranged proper arrangements for collecting and disposing of waste materials?
- Is the work area and interior adequately lit? Have we sufficient additional lighting provided when work is carried on after dark or inside buildings?

SCAFFOLDS

- Are all of our scaffolds and work platforms erected, altered and dismantled by competent persons?
- Do we have handover certificates for all work platforms and scaffolds?
- Is there safe access method (ladder) to the scaffold platform?
- Have all uprights been provided with base plates (and, where necessary, timber sole plates) or prevented in some other way from slipping or sinking?
- Are all of the uprights, ledgers, braces and struts in position?
- Is the scaffold secured to the building or structure in enough places to prevent collapse?
- Are there adequate guardrails and toe boards or an equivalent standard of protection at every edge from which a person could fall 2 m or more?
- Are intermediate guardrails fitted?

Where Guard Rails and Toe Boards or Similar are Used:

- Are the toe boards at least 150 mm in height?
- Is the upper guardrail positioned at a height of at least 910 mm above the work area?
- Are additional precautions, e.g., intermediate guard rails or brick guards in place to ensure that there is

no unprotected gap of more than 470 mm between the toe board and upper guard rail?

- Are the working platforms fully boarded and are the boards arranged to avoid tipping or tripping?
- Are there effective barriers or warning notices in place to stop people using an incomplete scaffold, e.g., where working platforms are not fully boarded?
- Has the scaffold been designed and constructed to cope with the materials stored on it and are these distributed evenly?
- Does a competent person inspect the scaffold regularly, e.g., at least once a week; always after it has been substantially altered, damaged and following extreme weather?
- Are the results of inspections recorded in our company records or site diary?

POWERED ACCESS EQUIPMENT

- Has the equipment been erected by a competent person?
- Is fixed equipment, e.g., mast climbers, rigidly connected to the structure against which it is operating?
- Does our working platform have adequate guard rails and toe boards or other barriers to prevent people and materials falling off?
- Have precautions been taken to prevent people being struck by the moving platform, projections from the building or falling materials, e.g., barrier or fence around the base?
- Are our operators or subcontractors trained and competent to use this equipment?

- Are the power supply isolated and the equipment secured at the end of the working day?

LADDERS

- Are ladders we have supplied the right means of access for this project or job?
- Are all of the ladders used by us and our sub-contractors in good condition?
- Have we secured them to prevent them slipping sideways or outwards?
- Do our ladders sections raise a sufficient height above their landing place? If not, are there other hand-holds available?
- Are our ladders positioned so that users do not have to over-stretch or climb over obstacles to work?
- Does the ladder being inspected rest against a solid surface and not on fragile or insecure materials?

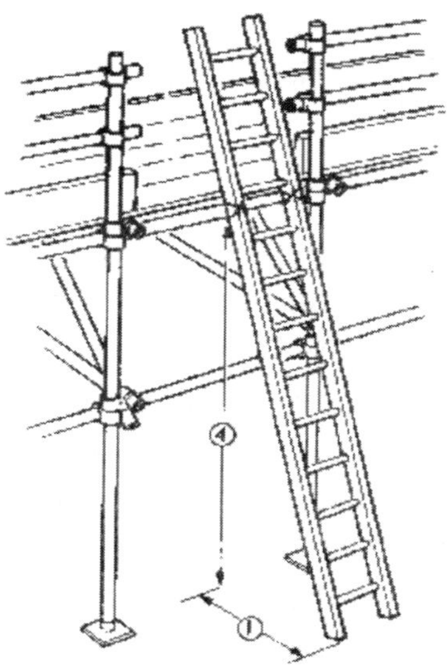

ROOF WORK

- Are there enough barriers and is there other edge protection to stop people or materials falling from roofs?
- Are harnesses available for the workforce if required?
- Do the roof battens provide safe hand and foot holds? If not, are crawling ladders or boards provided and used?
- During industrial roofing, are precautions taken to stop people falling from the leading edge of the roof or from fragile or partially fixed sheets, which could give way?
- Are suitable barriers, guardrails or covers, etc. provided where people pass or work near fragile material such as asbestos cement sheets and roof lights?
- Are crawling boards provided where work on fragile materials cannot be avoided?
- Are people excluded from the area below the roof work? If this is not possible, have additional precautions been taken to stop debris falling onto them?

EXCAVATIONS

- Is an adequate supply of timber, trench sheets, props or other supporting material made available before excavation work begins?
- Is this material strong enough to support the sides?
- Is a safe method used for putting in the support, i.e., one that does not rely on people working within an unsupported trench?
- If the sides of the excavation are sloped back or battered, is the angle of batter sufficient to prevent collapse?

- Is there safe access to the excavation, e.g., by a sufficiently long, secured ladder?
- Are there guardrails or other equivalent protection to stop people falling in?
- Are properly secured stop blocks provided to prevent tipping vehicles falling in?
- Does the excavation affect the stability of neighboring structures?
- Are materials, spoil or plant stored away from the edge of the excavation in order to reduce the likelihood of a collapse of the side?
- Is the excavation inspected by a competent person at the start of every shift; and after any accidental collapse or event likely to have affected its stability?

MANUAL HANDLING

- Has the risk of manual handling injuries been assessed?
- Are hoists, telehandlers, wheel-barrows and other plant or equipment used so that manual lifting and handling of heavy objects is kept to a minimum?
- Are materials such as cement ordered in 25 kg bags?
- Can our team avoid the handling of heavy blocks?

HOISTS

- Is our hoist protected by a substantial enclosure to prevent someone from being struck by any moving part of the hoist or falling down the hoist way?
- Are gates provided at all landings, including ground level?

- Are the gates kept shut except when the platform is at the landing?
- Are the controls arranged so that the hoist can be operated from one position only?
- Are the hoist operators or sub-contractors trained and competent?
- Is the hoist's safe working load clearly marked?
- If the hoist is for materials only, is there a warning notice on the platform or cage to stop people riding on it?
- Is the hoist inspected weekly, and thoroughly examined every six months by a competent person?
- Are the results of inspection recorded?

CRANES AND LIFTING APPLIANCES

- Is the mobile or static crane working on a firm level base?
- Are the safe working loads and corresponding radii known and considered before any lifting begins?
- If the crane has a capacity of more than one tone, does it have an automatic safe load indicator that is maintained and inspected weekly?
- Are all operators trained and competent?
- Has the banksman/slinger/signaller been trained to give signals and to attach loads correctly?
- Do the operator and signaler/banks man find out the weight and centre of gravity of the load before trying to lift it?
- Are cranes inspected weekly, and thoroughly examined every 14 months by a competent person?

- Are the results of inspections and examinations recorded?
- Does the crane have a current test certificate?

PLANT AND MACHINERY

- Is the right plant and machinery being used for the job? Have the entire project team agreed on this point?
- Are all-dangerous parts guarded, e.g., exposed gears, chain drives, projecting engine shafts?
- Are guards secured and in good repair?
- Is the machinery maintained in good repair and are all safety devices operating correctly?
- Are all operators trained and competent?

TRAFFIC AND VEHICLES

- Have separate pedestrian, vehicle access points and routes around the site been provided? If not, are vehicles and pedestrians kept separate wherever possible?
- Have one-way systems or turning points been provided to minimize the need for reversing?
- Where vehicles have to reverse, are they controlled by properly trained banks man?
- Are vehicles maintained; do the steering, handbrake and footbrake work properly? Have drivers received proper training?
- Are vehicles securely loaded?
- Are passengers prevented from riding in dangerous positions?

FIRE AND EMERGENCIES

General

- Have emergency procedures been developed, e.g., evacuating the site in case of fire or rescue from a confined space?
- Are people on site aware of the procedures?
- Is there a means of raising the alarm and does it work?
- Are there adequate escape routes and are these kept clear?

Fire

- Is the quantity of flammable material on site kept to a minimum?
- Are there provided proper storage areas for flammable liquids and gases, e.g., LPG and acetylene?
- Are containers and cylinders returned to these stores at the end of the shift?
- If liquids are transferred from their original containers are the new containers suitable for flammable materials?
- Is smoking banned in areas where gases or flammable liquids are stored and used? Are other ignition sources also prohibited?
- Are our gas cylinders and associated equipment in good condition?
- When gas cylinders are not in use, are the valves fully closed?
- Are cylinders stored outside?
- Are adequate bins or skips provided for storing waste?
- Is flammable and combustible waste removed regularly?
- Are the right number and type of fire extinguishers available and accessible?

HAZARDOUS SUBSTANCES

- Have we considered all harmful materials, e.g., asbestos, lead, solvents, paints etc. and have we identified them properly?
- Have the risks to everyone who might be exposed to these substances been assessed?
- Have precautions been identified and put in place, e.g., is protective equipment provided and used; are workers and others who are not protected kept away from exposure?

Noise

- Are breakers and other plant or machinery fitted with silencers?
- Are barriers erected to reduce the spread of noise?
- Is work sequenced to minimize the number of people exposed to noise?
- Are others not involved in the work kept away?
- Is suitable hearing protection provided and worn in noisy areas?

Welfare

- Have suitable and sufficient numbers of toilets been provided and are they kept clean?
- Are there clean washbasins, warm water, soap and towels?
- Is suitable clothing provided for those who have to work in wet, dirty or otherwise adverse conditions?
- Are there facilities for changing, drying and storing clothes?
- Is drinking water provided?
- Is there a site hut or other accommodation where workers can sit, make tea and prepare food?

- Is there adequate first aid provision?
- Are welfare facilities easily and safely accessible to all who need to use them?

PROTECTIVE CLOTHING

- Has adequate personal protective equipment, e.g., hard hats, safety boots, gloves, goggles, and dust masks been provided?
- Is the equipment in good condition and worn by all who need it?

ELECTRICITY

- Is the supply voltage for tools and equipment the lowest necessary for the job (could battery operated tools and reduced voltage systems, e.g., 110 V or even lower in wet conditions, be used)?
- Where mains voltage has to be used, are trip devices, e.g., Residual Current Devices (RCDs) provided for all equipment?
- Are RCDs protected from damage, dust and dampness and checked daily by users?
- Are cables and leads protected from damage by sheathing, protective enclosures or by positioning away from causes of damage?
- Are all connections to the system properly made and are suitable plugs used?
- Is there an appropriate system of user checks, formal visual examinations by site managers and combined inspection and test by competent persons for all tools and equipment?

- Are scaffolders, roofers etc. or cranes or other plant, working near or under overhead lines? Has the electricity supply been turned off or have other precautions, such as 'goal posts' or taped markers been provided to prevent them contacting the lines?
- Have underground electricity cables been located (with a cable locator and cable plans), marked and precautions for safe digging been taken?

PROTECTING THE PUBLIC

- Are the public fenced off or otherwise protected from the work?
- When work has stopped for the day?
- Are the gates secured?
- Is the perimeter fencing secure and undamaged?
- Are all ladders removed or their rungs boarded so that they cannot be used?
- Are excavations and openings securely covered or fenced off?
- Is all plant immobilized to prevent unauthorized use?
- Are bricks and materials safely stacked?
- Are flammable or dangerous substances locked away in secure storage places?

❒ ❒ ❒

CHAPTER 3

Safety in Core Construction Activities

INTRODUCTION

Construction industry needs to give utmost importance to the safety aspects of their fellow workers and expects full co-operation from all in the task of total safety.

Safety is not the responsibility of only safety department or the officers. It is workers responsibility also. It is a combined effort directed to the well being of everybody connected to construction work. All are in it when it comes to the matter of safety.

Unsafe and thoughtless act may lead to accident and injury resulting in suffering not only to the worker but to the members of their families also.

Unsafe act of any body may also cause accident and injury to those working with or near and may also result in damage to machines and equipments.

When accidents take place, project and construction suffers. An accident is a loss to the worker, the project and to nation as well.

The safety aspects involved during project construction phase are different from those during regular operation and maintenance phase.

During various stages of project construction, different hazards gain significance. For example during civil works, collapses of structures are not unlikely. During erection work; falling of persons from heights, failure of cranes/slings, falling of equipment, fires caused during welding etc. are possible. During testing/commissioning; electrically caused shocks/ fires/explosions are quite possible. During storage of equipment prior to erection, fire hazards are possible. The possible hazards during project construction are:

- Accidents due to pit fall in trench, excavation.
- Fall of persons from heights.
- Accidents due to failure of cranes, slings, ropes, D-shackles etc.
- Out brake of fire.
- Falling of objects on human body.
- Road accidents.
- Collapse of structures, walls and slabs.
- Electric shocks.
- Explosions/fires.
- Equipment failures.
- Lightning strokes.
- Flashovers.
- Unsafe equipment.

The safety management during construction phase of the project aims at zero accident and hundred percent safeties.

Field/site quality management ensures good quality of site work at every stage of construction. Good field quality ensures higher reliability and safety of the plant and equipment during operation. Construction quality has long term effect on safety. Poor quality during construction enhance possibilities of equipment failure, fire hazards and accidents during regular operation of the plant and equipment.

Good quality construction is very essential and important. Project construction activities include:

- Receiving of equipment, storage.
- Civil works.
- Installation.
- Testing – commissioning.
- Energizing.
- Trial operations.
- Handing over to operating staff.

Safety of personnel and plant is very important during the entire period of construction. The hazards during construction phase include pitfalls, fall of objects, and failure of construction equipment, fires, road accidents, collapse of civil construction, electric shocks, electric flashovers, explosions, equipment failures etc.

Construction site should have safety organizations and written safety procedures. By following safety procedures, accidents and losses can be minimized and safety can be ensured. Good field quality ensures safety during subsequent phases of project.

For example:

- Good civil work – safety during erection.
- Good erection – safety during commissioning.
- Good commissioning – safety during operation.
- Good operations – safety of personnel.

Good quality of construction goes a long way towards safety of personnel and plant during subsequent operations of the plant.

Main Activities During Construction of a Project Include

- Receiving and storage of construction materials
- Civil works: foundations, super structures, roads, trenches, fencing, structures, control room, buildings, administrative building, auxiliary building etc.
- Installation (erection) work: earthing system, galvanized steel structure, overload shielding system equipment, transformers, generators, motors, power cables, control cables, stationary auxiliaries.
- Testing of equipment, auxiliaries, sub-systems.
- Pre-commissioning tests on sub-systems.
- Final commissioning and energizing, trial operation.
- Operation and maintenance.

The objectives of field quality and safety during construction are:

- To ensure excellent quality of work during every stage of the project construction.
- To ensure that the personnel and plant are safe during construction and during regular plant operation and maintenance.
- The plant and its equipment give long, trouble free and safe service with minimum down time/maximum efficiency, lowest cost, and with good environment.

Field Quality and Safety Manager to Ensure

Field quality and safety are ensured at every stage of construction. Activities are done properly with excellent quality and full safety. Troubles are attended promptly and safely. Permanent solutions are found and it is ensured that it should not repeat again. Field quality system is formulated, enforced and monitored. Awareness about field quality and safety are created. Human resources are developed for field work quality and safety. Records are maintained in master documentation and working documentation room.

Hazards Due to Poor Field Quality

Poor civil work results in collapse of buildings, breaking of roads, seepage/leakage of water through roof/side walls, clogging of water in cable trenches, clogging of water in yards, tilting of yard structures, difficulties in erection, permanent difficulty in the plant, poor working environment, unsafe working conditions.

Poor erection quality, defects in equipment/plant results in: frequent failures, frequent faults, fire, unsafe working conditions, electrical shocks, accidents due to mechanical/ structural/electrical failure.

Poor testing and commissioning results in frequent failures of equipment. All such hazards can be prevented by enforcing field quality and safety procedures at site during construction period.

Unsafe Conditions and Acts During and After Project Construction

- Accidents due to pitfalls in trench, excavations and during civil and installation work.
- Fall of persons from heights, during civil and installation work.
- Accidents due to failure of cranes, slings, ropes, d-shackles etc. while receiving and storage and during installation.
- Fires during receiving and storage, installations, testing and commissioning and operation.
- Falling of objects on human body during civil work, installation and maintenance.
- Road accidents during receiving and storage of materials, civil work and installation.

- Collapse of structures, walls and slabs during civil works and installations.
- Electric shocks during civil work, installation and testing and commissioning and maintenance.
- Explosions/fires during testing and commissioning and operation.
- Equipment failures during testing and commissioning and operation.
- Lightening strokes during civil works, installation and operation.
- Flash over during testing and commissioning and operation.
- Unsafe equipment during operation and maintenance.

General Safety Facilities to be Provided at Construction Sites Lighting Facility

Construction site premises must be well illuminated to prevent tripping in pit falls, accidents and thefts. Areas which need lighting include:

- Roads fence and gates.
- Storage areas and access areas.
- Loading platforms/unloading platforms.
- Excavations, trenches.
- Concreting platforms.
- Semi finished pillars, slabs.
- Switch yards.
- Super structures of buildings of each floor.

Material Handling and Storage Facilities

- Highest loads on slabs occur during construction of building. Temporary supports to slabs under construction should be strong enough to prevent collapse due to own weight.

- The rigging equipment for material handling, unloading, loading, erection such as ropes, chains, wire ropes, nylon ropes must be inspected before every working shift. Worn out ropes, chains etc. must be scrapped.
- Scrap must be removed from construction site and disposed off promptly.
- Packing materials should be disposed off quickly and must not be allowed to remain at construction site. Packaging material presents fire hazard.
- When material is to be dropped from height greater than 10 meter, enclosures should be provided to prevent falling of dust and objects beyond safe zone.

Personal Protective Equipments Facilities at Construction Site

- Hard hats to prevent head injury due to falling objects.
- Ear- muffs/ear-plugs for protection of hearing system from loud sound.
- Eye and face protection for welders, riveters and grinders.
- Safety belts and safety harnesses to prevent fall from heights during civil work, erection work and maintenance work.
- Fire protection during construction.
- Tested metallic tools.
- Electrical tools with insulating handles for working on low voltage circuits.
- Strong reliable ladders with protection rings.
- Vertical railings around pits and cable trenches.
- Horizontal scaffolds supported by ropes, structures for civil/erection works. Types of scaffolds include: (1) welded frames (2) tube and coupled scaffolds (3) suspension scaffolds and (4) wire rope scaffolds.

- Cut-outs in floor must be covered by a slab or by strong fabricated steel mesh to prevent pit falls.

Fire Fighting Facility During Construction

Adequate fire fighting facility must be available at site during construction period for storage, civil works, erection, testing work etc. Fires can occur in stores area or at construction site due to electrical flash over/faults, welding sparks, sparks in temporary electrical switch boards, open flames carried by construction workers, lightening etc. Fire extinguishers, fire hydrants, mobile fire fighting tenders, should be available to prevent loss due to fire during construction and subsequent operation stage.

CIVIL CONSTRUCTION ACTIVITIES

Civil construction activities mainly involve:

- Site clearance.
- Storage of construction materials.
- Excavation.
- Shuttering and shoring.
- Demolition and removal of debris.

Safety in Site Clearance

- Safe place for keeping the materials to be selected.
- Either material to be properly stacked or to be shifted to appropriate place.
- If any electrical connection or service connections are interfering with the site clearance job, they are to be diverted in consultation with appropriate authority.
- Approach to the place of work should be cleared and preferably approach should be provided at least two sides, so that in case of any interference in one side the job is not disturbed.

STORAGE OF CONSTRUCTION MATERIALS

1. All materials are to be stacked properly. The stack height should not exceed 4 ft. above ground level.
2. Safe approach to be provided and maintained from individual stack to place of work. Stacking of materials should not disturb handling mechanical, structural or electrical materials stacked nearby.
3. No stack of materials should rest against any structure or building wall.
4. Construction materials should not be kept on the edge of the pits and excavated area.
5. Clear passages to be provided to the workers.
6. Proper drainage to be provided so that the discharge of water, used for washing of materials etc., flow into the pits or make the ground surface slushy.
7. Boxes, pallets, containers, ropes, pulleys, used for handling and transporting stacked materials to be checked periodically.
8. Proper care should be taken for nails while stacking dismantled planks.

Excavation Safety, Some Definitions

'Excavation' means any man made cut, cavity, trench or depression in an earth surface, formed by earth removal.

'Confined space' in relation to excavation is a space that, by design and/or configuration has:

1. Limited openings for entry and exit.
2. May contain or produce hazardous substances.
3. Unfavorable natural ventilation.
4. Is not intended for continuous employee occupancy.

'Trench' in relation to excavation means a narrow excavation (in relation to its length) made below the surface of the ground.

1. In general, the depth is greater than the width, but the width of a trench (measured at the bottom) is not greater than 15 ft. (4.6 m).
2. If forms or other structures are installed or constructed in an excavation so as to reduce the dimension measured from the forms or structure to the side of the excavation to 15 ft. (4.6 m) or less (measured at the bottom of the excavation), the excavation is also considered as a trench.

'Accepted engineering practices' are procedures that are compatible with the standard practice required of a registered professional engineer.

'Adjacent structure stability' refers to the stability of the foundations of adjacent structures whose locations may create surcharges, changes in soil conditions, or other disruptions that have the potential to extend into the failure of the excavation trench.

'A competent person' is one who is capable of identifying existing and predictable hazards in the surroundings, or working conditions which are unsanitary, hazardous or dangerous to employees, and has authorization to eliminate them.

A competent person must have specific training in, and be knowledgeable about, soil analysis, and the use of protective systems.

'Protective system' refers to a method of protecting employees from cave ins, material that could fall or roll from an excavations, face into an excavation, and from the collapse of adjacent structures.

Protective system includes support systems, sloping and benching systems, shield systems and other systems that provide the necessary protection.

SAFETY WHILE EXCAVATION

1. Excavation area should be barricaded.
2. Excavated material should be thrown at least 2 ft. from the edge of the excavated area.
3. Excavated material should not be allowed to accumulate in a busy work area, it should be removed promptly.
4. If work is to continue in night, lighting should be provided around the barricading.
5. Location of underground water pipes, gas pipes, fuel pipes, storage tanks, electric cables, telephone lines, should be ascertained by competent authority before commencing excavation of area. The locations should be marked clearly.
6. Adequate protection must be provided for underground pipes, cables, telephone lines, tanks etc.
7. No shovel, crane or dragline should be used to excavate near electric lines. Power should be shut off while excavating near them.
8. If excavation is being done by means of picks or paving breakers, care should be taken not be puncture any cable or service line. Preferably shut down of these lines should be taken while excavating near them or they should be well protected.
9. Adequate suspension or support should be provided for hanging lines, pipes etc.
10. If any excavation is to carried out in proximity of any structure, where it is likely to sink/collapse, temporary

supports to be provided to transfer the load of the structure to a firm ground before excavation.

11. Any blasting if required to be done, it should be as per the rules and regulations.
12. Any surcharge like sloping ground, track line, building or machine structural if found within 45 degree from the bottom edge of the pit to be excavated. Care should be taken to retain the surcharge load.
13. Heavy structures or the machines to be erected should not be kept within 45 degrees line from the bottom edge of the pit.
14. Any crack of ground near the excavated pit if noticed during the work in the pit in progress, the work must be stopped immediately and brought to the attention of appropriate authority. No body should be allowed to work there till preventive measures taken.
15. Open excavation adjacent to and lower than wall foundations or other footings, structural columns etc. should be executed by experienced worker with the knowledge of soil. Special care should be taken to prevent undercutting in reclaimed or filled on soils.
16. When excavation is to be done within a building precautions have to be taken for the existing installations, structures, foundations etc.
17. A trench of 4 ft. or more deep should be provided with ladders. Stair ways or ramps, so spaced that no worker in the trench should be more than 50 ft. from one of them. Ladders should extend at least 3 ft. above the ground.
18. Pick and shovel men while excavation should keep at a safe distance.
19. While excavating on the slope whose height is over 10 ft. men should use safety belt.

20. The sides of trenches more than 4 ft. deep, shoring with timber should be done, where they are slopped to the angle of repose or unless the trench is in solid rock.

EXCAVATION INSPECTIONS

Daily inspection of excavations, the adjacent areas, and protective systems shall be made by a competent person for evidence of a situation that could result in:

- Possible cave-ins.
- Indication of failures of protective systems.
- Hazardous atmospheres.
- Other hazardous conditions.

Inspection shall be conducted prior to the start of work and as needed throughout the shift.

SHUTTERING AND SHORING

1. In case the soil is soft, loose, the bonding is loose, the water sippage is observed. Shoring of adequate strength has to be provided during excavation. Shoring also to be done below 4 ft. depth of trench.
2. Subsoil water accumulation should be pumped out from the excavation area. If slippage of soil is observed, then it should be projected by proper shoring or putting sand bags.
3. Inflow of water should be diverted away from the area.
4. Undercutting of the soil should be avoided. In case the soil is undercut proper propping should be provided to support the hangovers.
5. Proper cribbing of support to be done as specified/ instructed by the appropriate authority if excavation is done below or close to railway track.

6. If undercutting is necessary, then shoring with proper propping should be done as specified or instructed by competent authority.
7. Wooden planks or steel sheets of adequate strength should be used for shuttering
8. Planks or sheets should be rigidly fixed with one another by means of clamps, hooks or nails. The joint should be sufficiently strong to take care of load.
9. Props used to support the shuttering should be of adequate strength.
10. While dismantling shuttering persons working below should be alerted.
11. The vertical props should rest on firm base.
12. After completion of the job, the shuttering should not left for long time.

DEMOLITION AND REMOVAL OF DEBRIS

1. Before demolishing a building or structure either protect or disconnect the utility services (gas, steam, and electricity etc.).
2. Remove all fragile and hanging materials from inside the building.
3. The area should be cordoned and barricaded. Caution boards and red flags should be displayed at places. The distance of cordoning will depend on the height at which demolition is taking place.
4. Chutes or container cages should be used to lower down debris.
5. Proper and tested tackle to be used while lowering heavy materials.
6. An experienced supervisor should give signal and supervise.

7. The cages, hoists, tackles, should not be overloaded.
8. Debris should be removed at earliest.
9. Safe and easy approach to be provided for quick transport.
10. Water should be sprayed to control dust wherever required.
11. Trucks should not be overloaded or materials should not spill on the way.
12. Materials should not project beyond side or back panels of truck.
13. Before demolishing building with overhung chhajas etc. they should be properly supported or demolished first before demolishing super structure of the building.

Structural and Mechanical Erection Activities

Structural Erection

1. The structural members should be kept in orderly manner on the ground so that they do not roll down or slide while being handled.
2. The structural member should be able to be taken out as per sequence of erection without disturbing the stack at the same time light structural should not be stacked below heavy structural where they are likely to be damaged.
3. Clear passages to be left for easy handling and transportation of structures.
4. Plates and structural should be stacked separately. Also loose materials should not be stacked with heavy materials.
5. While removing any materials from the stack care should be taken not to disturb remaining materials of the stack.

6. Safety appliances should be used regularly as per instruction.
7. Suitable scaffolding should be prepared for working safely. No scaffolding should be overloaded.
8. Safe approaches to be provided to the scaffolding.
9. While work is proceeding on scaffolding, roofs or other elevated places precautions must be taken to prevent labor going underneath to avoid injury due to falling object.
10. The area below where work is going on should be cordoned.
11. No loose materials to be kept over the scaffolding.
12. No materials should be dropped on the ground from a height; instead they should be properly tied and lowered. Loose materials, e.g., muck, debris etc. should be lowered by filling in gunny bag.
13. Proper signaling arrangement to be made where lifting tackle/crane is used.
14. Tools for example spanner etc. riveting hammer etc. should be tied with a rope fixed so that they will drop on the ground in case of any slip.
15. While using jack care should be taken to provide wooden block both at the top and at the base of the jack. Also the jack should be tied by means of rope to prevent slippage of jack.
16. If hydraulic jack is used, the load lifting should rest on wooden block or temporary structure to prevent mishap due to failure of jack.
17. Only those persons who are skilled in working at height to be engaged for job to be done at height. Persons suffering from diseases, e.g., epilepsy, blood-pressure etc. and addicted to drug, alcohol etc. should not be allowed to work at height.

18. Where the job demands physical exertion or working near gas line, hot atmosphere should be regularly changed to avoid fatigue.
19. Care must be taken to fasten the erection members properly and secured by guys etc. whenever necessary.
20. Written clearance to be taken from appropriate authority while working near gas line, live electric line, crane gantry etc. the clearance to be returned in writing after completing the job and removing all men working near the area.
21. For working near live electric line, the program should be discussed with operation department, safety department, electric department and other concerned department if any. An agreed procedure to be decided for doing the job. The clearance to be taken in writing. In case of electric shock immediate first-aid, e.g., artificial respiration to be resorted to.
22. If job to be carried out in crane gantry, agreed procedure to be worked out in consultation with electrical, operation and safety department. Stop blocks to be provided on the gantry on either side at a distance about 20 ft. from working area. In addition red flag (or at night red light) to be provided to caution the crane driver about men working on the crane gantry. All men working on the crane gantry should be given induction regarding hazards due to clearances of the building etc. Caution boards wherever required to be provided in appropriate places.
23. Job to be carried out near gas line, steam line etc. the program to be discussed with operating department, safety department, energy and economy and any other departments concerned and agreed procedures to be worked out. Clearance to be taken in writing in the

specified form and to be returned after the job is over. Services of fire brigade and compressor to provide sufficient fresh air to be done wearing gas mask or regular testing arrangement to be made for detection of gas leakage. After the job is over the clearance to be returned in writing.

24. While lifting structural, weight to be approximately ascertained and proper lifting tackle of appropriate capacity to be selected.
25. Guy ropes to be used while handling heavy materials.
26. Ropes and slings should be protected by providing padding over sharp edges.
27. Slinging should be done such a way to prevent the load from slipping.
28. All people should use proper safety appliances.
29. Proper sequence of erection to be followed.
30. Any specific note from the designer/supplier should be followed.
31. Gas cylinders should not be dropped or dragged on the ground. Acetylene (Dissolved Acetylene) cylinder should be kept in vertical position. Lifting magnet or chain should not be used for handling cylinders. Cylinders should be kept away from all sources of contamination, e.g., oil, batteries, fire etc. and heat. Cylinder valve should not be lubricated. Care should be taken not to give additional leverage for opening cylinder valves, which likely damage it.
32. In structures where provision, e.g., expansion, free movement etc. are provided, they should be checked properly.

Mechanical Erection

1. All precautions pertaining to structural job should be followed.

2. Load to be properly ascertained and position of centre of gravity and load transfer at slinging point to be thought of before handling any equipment.
3. A special check is required regarding fitness of all lifting and haulage tackles, ropes, slings etc.
4. Selection of tommy bars, rollers, skids etc. should be selected depending on the type of equipment to be handled.
5. The common tendency of checking gear meshing, lubrication, coupling matching, and hole matching etc. by feeling with a finger must be strictly curbed.
6. Gas cutting of any member should be avoided.
7. In case of all installation to be tested and tried, the supplier's instructions should be properly studied and followed during installation and testing.
8. A general check on integral or other service system, lubrication system, and check on free and easy movement of all moving parts and their safe clearance to be taken care before such test.
9. All safety features to be checked.
10. Regulations, e.g., boiler regulation, regulation for explosives, electricity rule etc. and any other set procedure, e.g., working near gas line, electric line etc. should be followed.
11. Attention should be paid to all mechanical safety guards, toe-boards, hand railings, hatch-way covers, ladders etc.
12. Grinding wheels should be handled with care. These should be visually inspected/checked by ringing test for possible damage before mounting. Wheels should be covered by guard at least one half of the grinding wheel and operator should use safety goggles. Wheels

should not be tampered for mounting and no materials should be ground for which the wheels are not designed for.

13. If work is to be carried out over fragile roof, all men required to work on the roof top should be trained for safe work on the roof too. Crawling boards should be made use of during any work on fragile roof top. Also, caution boards should be fixed up at ladders leading to the roof top – "danger do not go on the roof top without permission."
14. Eye bolts fixed at correct slinging points for heavy machinery parts, motors, generators, turbines etc. should be utilized for handling.
15. Torque wrenches are provided for taking the correct strain during tightening of nuts on bolts.
16. Suppliers' instruction should be strictly followed for special installation, e.g., fixing of friction grip bolts etc.
17. Safety valves for steam, compressed air and gas requirement and expansion joints should be checked.
18. No slings should be overloaded. Safe working load charts should be followed for slings.
19. Proper quality of pulley block should be used. In no case pulley block suitable for fiber rope should be used for steel wire rope.

ELECTRICAL

1. Indian Electricity rules to be followed.
2. Wires of proper size and of proper insulation to be used.
3. It is preferable not to use loose and temporary wiring even for power supply for lighting, machine or to any electrical equipment.

4. All electrical equipments, switches, machines, welding machines, drilling machines, etc., should be properly grounded.
5. Voltage and current rating should be prominently displayed at the installations.
6. No rewirable fuses to be used. Instead HRC fuses to be used for all power connections.
7. Caution boards should be properly displayed and marking of individual switches to be made.
8. All electric lines should be drawn at least above man's height. No live wire should be laid on the ground or wet surface. All electric joints should be properly insulated.
9. Electrical installation should be protected from water and direct flame.
10. Only competent persons should make electrical connections and installations and attend electrical defects. It is essential to ensure that they are not only capable of executing/supervising the job but they also have the necessary competency certificate as per statutory requirement.
11. While using arc welding machine, safety rules laid down should be followed scrupulously. Code of practice for safe use of arc welding equipment should be followed.
12. Selection of right safety appliances, tools, materials and instruments for particular jobs must be pre-planned.
13. Materials and equipment of correct quality should be used, e.g., asbestos insulated cables for hot locations, flame proof fittings, switch gear, motors etc., for oil, gas and other inflammable installation areas where there are hazards of explosion, totally enclosed fan

cooled motors in damp and corrosive surroundings, water proof fittings for underwater installation, etc.

14. Complete understanding and co-ordination should be pre-arranged with staff authorized to give clearance and staff supervising the job. Particular care should be taken in case of multiple sources of supply to see that all sources are made dead and all grounding precautions and tests are done before work commences. Clearances should be exchanged in writing in standard form.
15. Before energizing any installation, testing of the insulation resistances of individual units, proper phasing out and voltage tests, performance of protective and control system, checking of earth resistance of the whole system, checking connection, making and tagging should be carried out. Safety appliances, e.g., rubber gloves, rubber mat, grounding rod, neon tester, insulated screw driver, and pliers etc., should be used. Installations should be energized only after taking necessary clearance from the appropriate authority.
16. Limit switches, inter locks, etc., if provided, should be checked before commissioning any equipment.

General

Scaffolding and Approaches

1. Common types of scaffolds used are:
   (a) Partially fabricated steel scaffolds in welded steel tubular frames with removable cross bracings of proper design.
   (b) Complete tubular steel scaffolds about 50 mm. O.D. and length 2 m to 4 m with special clamps and couplers.

(c) Temporary wood scaffolds of sizes 1 m × 1/2 m to 2 m × 1 m in which the decking planks are nailed to wooden beams below and the scaffold is suspended by four pieces of wire rope/rope strand of over 6 mm. dia. Or fiber rope of 15 mm dia.

(d) Corrugated sheets (22 gauge or thicker) placed over pipe or structural tied up by wire rope or wire rope strands of at least 6 mm. dia. is very common. Both ends of corrugated sheets should be properly tied and overhung should be restricted to 150 mm.

(e) Special fabricated cages of suitable design for chimney repair/painting skip rail changing etc.

(f) Bamboo scaffolds should be made out of double bamboo of good quality over 75 mm should be paired together by fastening with rope.

2. All scaffolds should be cross braced to prevent its movement. Wooden scaffolds runners should be bolted with vertical props. All joints of one member to another should be sufficiently strong.

3. All scaffolds should be provided with toe-boards of 150 mm height and side hand railings of 900 mm height.

4. Scaffolds should not be erected near live electric wire, gas line or fire. Scaffoldings should be made either with 18″ × 2″ thick planks or corrugated sheets, the planks or sheets should not be extended beyond the supporting pipes by more than 8″. Planks or sheets should either be clamped or tied with coir rope and thicker gauge wire. All scaffolds should be provided with side railings and toe-boards.

5. Proper and safe approach to be provided to scaffolds. Dust or water should not accumulate over scaffolds.

6. All scaffolds must be checked from time to time and no scaffold to be overloaded. Scaffolds should be designed to take at least 50% overload for safety.

7. Where ladders are used for approach to scaffolds these should be securely fastened at top and bottom ends. The horizontal distance of the bottom leg from the vertical plane through top leg should be 1/4th of the length of the ladder. Ladders more than 10 ft. long should have man guard.
8. Where planks are used for approach to scaffolding these should be securely fastened at both ends and bamboo hand rails on each side of the walkway to be provided. Planks should not be less than 50 mm thick and should be of proper quality. In the inclined platform used as access, cross battens should be properly fixed at suitable distance depending on the slope to serve as footholds. Minimum head room of 2 m should be provided on all approaches. Width should be at least 900 mm.
9. No loose materials should be left over scaffolds.
10. All vertical props should rest on firm base.
11. Scaffolds should be horizontal. Padding of sharp edge by gunny bags, split pipes etc. should be done before tying ropes on the scaffold.
12. Scaffold should be dismantled early after completion of the job.

ROPES AND SLINGS

Safe Working Load

Ropes are broadly divided into fiber ropes, steel ropes, and synthetic ropes. First two categories are widely used. Safe working load of fiber rope (sisal) slings made out of steel ropes and use of 'V' clamps are given in the below chart.

Safe Load for Sisal Rope Blocks

Rope diameter	One part	Two parts	Three parts	Four parts
Inches	Tons	Tons	Tons	Tons
½″	0.11	0.20	0.27	0.32
¾″	0.22	0.40	0.54	0.66
1″	0.37	0.67	0.91	1.10

Care in Handling

The precautions which should be taken during use of ropes are as follows:

(a) All ropes used for construction purposes must be of good quality and of tested brand/supplier.

(b) Ropes should neither be kept on the floor nor should be kept in a closed box. These should be hung in loose coil of large dia. or to be wound in drum.

(c) Protection should be provided to ropes from weather, dampness, acid fumes, heat, chemicals etc.

(d) Avoid sharp edge, where the rope is likely to be damaged.

(e) Ropes should not be dragged on the ground.

(f) If fiber rope is used as grey rope for derrick, it should be loosened during rain, as it shrinks when it is wet.

(g) Periodically rope should be reversed.

(h) 'Whipping' of yarn is necessary to prevent opening out of strand.

(i) Ropes should be inspected before and after use.

INSTALLATIONS OF CROSSBY CLIPS

All clips must be placed with U bolt bearing on short or dead end of rope.

- *First* – tighten clip farthest end from eye.
- *Second* – put the clip nearest thimble and apply nut hand tight.
- *Third* – put on intermediate clips hand tight.
- *Fourth* – take a strain on the rope.
- *Fifth* – while the rope is under strain, tighten all clips.

A.B.C. of Fiber Rope Usage

1. Avoid kinks and twists.
2. Un-coil rope in correct direction.
3. Avoid overloading.
4. If wet, dry before storing
5. Never drag rope on floor.
6. Reverse rope ends periodically.
7. Inspect rope before and after use.
8. Reverse rope correctly on pulley blocks.
9. When used as slings do not pass over sharp edges.
10. Store on wooden platform or hang on wooden pegs.
11. Keep away from acid and chimney fumes.

Proof: Load = 2 × Safe Load

Safe Load for Wire-Rope Blocks

Wire diameter	Minimum diameter of sheaves	One part	Two parts	Three parts	Four parts	Five parts	Six parts
Inches	Inches	Tons	Tons	Tons	Tons	Tons	Tons
1/2″	8″	1.5	2.9	4.1	5.3	6.1	7.0
5/8″	10″	2.3	4.4	6.3	8.1	9.5	10.9
3/4″	12″	3.4	6.6	9.3	12.0	14.0	16.2
7/8″	14″	4.3	8.3	12.2	15.2	17.7	20.0
1″	16″	5.6	10.9	16.0	19.9	23.2	26.7

When to discard the rope:

(a) Discarded ropes should be destroyed.

(b) Frequently set for particular duly based on inspection and experience.

(c) Fiber ropes must be destroyed when powdery saw dust like substances comes out of the ropes.

(d) Reduction in diameter of ropes more than 8% for single layer and 5 to 6% in case of multiple layer ropes.

(e) Outline definitely loose or lost about 35% depth in case of single layer, 40% in case of multiple layer wire rope.

(f) Where the rope is subjected to severe load/shock load, lubrication of rope generally comes out from core.

(g) In a length of 8*d* (where '*d*' is the diameter of rope) the total visible broken ones exceed 10%.

(h) Where there is evidence of plastic wire and surface embrittleness.

(i) Rope subjected to severe corrosion or chemical action.

(j) Localized distortion or link.

(k) Sudden decrease of diameter.

(l) Collapsed core.

(m) One or more strands broken.

(n) Bird cage formed.

Safe Use of Construction Equipment and Tools

Hand Tools

1. These should be checked periodically by competent person and bad tools should be discarded.
2. Picks, hammer heads, files, screw drivers, shovels etc. should be provided with good handles made of approved quality of wood and tested for the purpose it is used.

3. The handle should be convenient for the grip and smooth. They should fit tightly with the implements.
4. Mushroom head chisel, hammers should be discarded.
5. Tools should be checked for any crack.
6. Wrenches, spanners which slip during use should be discarded.
7. Drills should be fastened to paving breaker to prevent its flying.

Pneumatic Compressor

1. Compressor should be checked for any crack in the air receiver and pipe connection. Air receiver should also be tested hydraulically by competent person and record should be maintained.
2. Safety valves should be checked periodically for their effectiveness.
3. Pressure gauges should be checked.
4. This should be installed/placed away from excavation.
5. Leakage in the pipeline should be avoided and air-hoses should be firmly clamped.
6. No one should use the compressed air to clean his dress or body. Compressed air should not be directed against any person.
7. Supply of compressed air to pneumatic tools should be controlled by valves. Bonding and tying of hoses should be avoided.

Pulleys

1. Proper quality and size of pulleys should be used. It should confirm standards as far as possible.
2. In no case pulley meant for fiber ropes should be used with steel ropes.

3. Sheaves, shafts, hook, hose pin, locking of pins should be checked before use.
4. Grooves of the sheaves should be uniform and smooth. The wire rope or fiber rope should run free without touching against the block or suspension parts.
5. Sheaves should rotate freely on the shaft.
6. The shaft should be free from crack and should not be worn-out.
7. Pins and hooks should not be worn out or unused.
8. Anchorage should be strong and firm.
9. Anti twister should be used to prevent rubbing of ropes against each other.

Chain Block and Chain Puller

1. Chain blocks/puller of proper lifting capacity should be used for lifting known loads.
2. Chain block/puller must be checked/tested periodically and to be inspected before use.
3. No cannibalisting (to repair with parts taken from other equipment) should be done on chain blocks.
4. Chain blocks/puller with fractured links, cracked links; if elongation of link more than 5% or interlink bearing more than 1/4″ should be discarded.
5. Chain blocks/puller should be tested for 'slip' by suspending safe load.
6. It should operate freely, and chain should not come out of pulleys.
7. The anchorage should be strong and rigid.
8. They should be checked for cracks, excessive wearing, elongation etc.
9. No chain block/puller which has been tempered in receiving arrangement, to be used unless it is thoroughly checked and tested by competent person.

10. Chain block/puller must be checked if stored for longer time, subjected to shock load, slipping of load, subjected to over loading, jamming of links etc. observed.

Winches

1. Safe working load with gearing arrangement should be marked on the winch and to be tested regularly.
2. Winch should not be over loaded.
3. It should be placed on a firm base and properly anchored.
4. The brake, ratchet arrangement, gear and pinion including thin meshing, wire rope including clamping arrangement. And direction of receiving rope drum, the rods should be used before using the winch.
5. Ratchet arrangement should be kept in position while hoisting a load.
6. The rods should be so adjusted not to allow drum movement causing clutch arrangement to slip.

Derricks

1. The lifting capacity of the derrick should be ascertained and it should be overloaded.
2. The mast, guy ropes, swivel hook, rope clips, strap blocks etc. of the derrick should be thoroughly checked befoe erecting the derrick.
3. Depending on the types of derrick, the mast should be firmly fixed by guy ropes/structure.
4. All precaution should be taken so that base of the derrick does not shift or shrink.
5. Guys of the derrick should be anchored tightly with strong structure/hold fasts.
6. The load being hoisted should not rub against the derrick.

Cranes

1. While using overhead crane/jib crane, the capacity of the crane should be ascertained. Brakes should be adjusted while lifting capacity load.
2. Crane should not be over loaded.
3. Mobile crane should be parked on hard soil or strong base. They should not be placed near the edge of the pit or excavation.
4. Safe working load of any mobile crane depends on:
   - Condition of ground.
   - Boom length.
   - Radius of rotation while lifting the load inclination of boom to the vertical.
   - Out rigger blocked/free.

   The safe working load is generally tabulated in the 'load chart' of the crane. Sometime the cranes are derated due to the structural condition, condition of clutch, brake etc.

   The load is the total load hung from the top sheaves of the boom including wt. of hook block etc.
5. Capacity marking should be displayed on the crane.
6. Only experienced persons should give signal to the crane operator. He should be more cautious while using more than one crane.
7. Stand signaling code/signals properly understood by the operator and signal man should be used.
8. Guy ropes should be used while hoisting heavy and bulky material.
9. The brake, boom, hook, wire ropes should be checked before using the crane for hoisting the materials.

10. The load being lifted should not touch the boom.
11. The boom or any part of the crane should not touch any live electric line/service line.
12. The boom should not be turned suddenly.
13. Jacks bearing (out-riggers) and rail clamp (for loco crane) should be used for handling bulky load, particularly at a lateral angle.
14. Proper quality of packing should be used and the out-rigger should rest tightly on the packing.
15. No body should stand below the boom or load.
16. The operator should be able to see the hook and load throughout the hoisting period.
17. Reeving (to fasten by reeving), clamping of ropes, hook blocks etc. should be checked before lifting the load.
18. Storm clamp or swing locks to be used while using the crane during storm.
19. At least two winding ropes should always be on the drum.

Jacks

1. Jacks should not be overloaded.
2. Manufacturers' instruction of use of jaws (particularly hydraulic gears) should be clear before use. Some hydraulic gears due to the position and construction of non-return valve are not used in horizontal and inclined position.
3. Load must rest on firm packing after lifting by you, before any body is allowed to move below the load.
4. Wooden blocks to be provided below and over the gick and the gick should be tied up by rope to prevent it from slipping.

5. Jacks of same capacity and type should be used while using a number of jacks simultaneously.
6. Inspect, clean, release the load after use.
7. Always use proper grade and clean oil. Standard lever for operating the jack as indicated by the supplier to be used.

SAFETY APPLIANCES

Safety appliances play a vital role in protecting the workman from injury during execution of job. Some of the important safety appliances are given below. They must be in good condition and conform to the laid down standard for them.

1. No worker should be allowed to work at construction job if he does not use fasteners.
2. Where work is carried out at different levels all must wear safety helmets.
3. Man working at heights must wear standard safety belts.
4. Persons doing handling jobs, gas cutting, welding or operating paving breakers should wear hand gloves prescribed for the job.
5. While gas cutting, brick dressing, welding, grinding, operating paving breakers, operating machines men must wear safety goggles recommended for the purpose.
6. Dust respirators should be provided to those workers engaged in brick cutting, breaking, dismantling concrete work, blasting etc.
7. Gas masks must be used while working near gas line or inside old redundant tunnel.
8. Ear plugs or ear muffs should be provided to those working at places with high sound level.

9. Apron should be used working near machine or handling chain etc.
10. Gum boots to be used while working with chemicals, acids etc.
11. Asbestos clothes, gloves to be used while handling hot objects.
12. No one should be allowed to use loose dress.
13. Fire fighting equipment of proper type to be used while working where there is chance of fire hazards.

Safety In Transport

1. Materials should be properly loaded considering its weight, dimension, capacity of the carrier, centre of gravity of load, clearance required for safety etc.
2. Load must be properly packed and lashed before transportation.
3. The truck, trailer and other transport vehicles should be in safe working conditions.
4. The power vehicles must have efficient brakes, warning hooters or horns and lights.
5. The tyres, the body, and deck should be in condition.
6. Properly spaced wooden battens or packing should be provided to prevent slipping of load.
7. The transport vehicles should not be overloaded. No material should project above the height of side panel or beyond the side panels. Materials may be allowed to project maximum 1 m at the back of the deck. Red caution should be displayed on the projected end.
8. The vehicle should not ply beyond the permissible speed limit.
9. The drivers should observe the timing during shift changing hours.

10. The driver should observe instruction for crossing the level crossing, over taking, taking turn etc.
11. None should get up or get down from a moving vehicle.
12. Men should not sit on the sides of the panels or on the top of drivers cabin.
13. Men should not sit near the load where there is possibility of rolling or shifting due to sudden application of brakes.
14. All must observe the road safety rules.
15. If material is transported in wagon, the route should be surveyed, so that the material will not foul with any fixed structure/object/another wagon while negotiating bends or turnouts.

Road Safety

1. The pedestrians, cyclists, drivers must follow the standard road safety rules framed for the purpose.
2. No body should try to cross the level crossing when drop gates are closed or signal is given for blocking the road. Stop, look, and proceed should be followed.
3. None should try to cross under the standing train or down the track where wagon is parked.
4. None should cross through the gap between buffers and wagons.
5. None should indulge in horse play while on the road.
6. Undue haste should be avoided on the road.
7. All warnings, cautions, instructions, “Do’s and Don’ts” of safety should be observed strictly by everyone.
8. All should be attentive while crossing.

Supervision

1. Duty of supervisor is to ensure safety of men and materials under him.

2. The supervisor should be thoroughly acquainted with surrounding areas, job to be done, risk involved, safety precautions needed, safety appliances required, first aid to be given etc.
3. The supervisor should train up his men in 'safety' related to the jobs they are to do and the site where they are to work. Also, he follows up to see that safety is ensured
4. The supervisor should check up from time to time the workmen, work areas, work methods and should try to rectify the defects in them.
5. He should posses' sufficient knowledge of the job and safety in the job to guide his men in the matter of safe execution of the job.
6. He should personally check safety appliances, scaffolds, tools and tackles periodically and should take appropriate action if needed.
7. The supervisor must take corrective measure in time for any violation of safety rules.
8. No worker should do a job of which he has not acquired sufficient working knowledge and appliances about the job.
9. In case of any injury, immediate first aid should be ensured by the supervisor.

Conclusion

Before work, check for safety, use safe metods and do not be hasty.

Is it safe?

One sure way to reduce accidents is to pin point unsafe situations or practices, so that the steps can be taken to correct them before any one gets hurt. An attempt has been made to identify some of the most elementary hazards found on sites, which frequently lead to accidents. The checklist is basic and should therefore be modified to suit local needs.

Safe Access

More than 50% of the accidents that keep people away from work involve falls or collisions of people, materials and vehicles. It is therefore vital that access from place to place be made safe.

Check Points

1. Is safe access provided for all on the site to reach their places of work, i.e., good roads, gang ways, passage ways, passenger hoists, stair cases, ladders and scaffolds?
2. Are all walkways level and free from obstruction?
3. Is the edge protection provided or other preventive measures taken where people are likely to fall from an open side?
4. Are holes and openings covered over with securely fixed covers or alternatively fenced off?
5. Is adequate lighting available when work has to continue after dark?
6. Is the site tidy and are materials stored in safe positions?
7. Are there proper arrangements for the gathering and disposal of the scrap?
8. Are the nails in the timber hammered down or removed?

Ladders

More accidents arise every year due to use and/or misuse of ladders than any other equipment.

Check Points

1. Is every ladder in good condition and free from obvious defects?
2. Are all the ladders secured near the top (including those used for short periods)?
3. If the ladder can not be secured near the top, is it secured near the bottom, weighted or footed?
4. Does the ladder rise at least 1 m above the place of landing? If not, is there adequate hand hold at the place of landing?
5. Are the ladders properly positioned for access?

Tubular Scaffolds

The law requires that scaffolding work be done with competent and experienced supervision. All scaffolders except trainees should be experienced and competent in their work. The loading for which a scaffold has been provided should be known. The loading should be evenly distributed. The scaffold should not be overloaded. Scaffolds are required to be inspected at least once a week and always after bad weather.

Check Points

1. Has proper access been provided to the scaffold platform?
2. Are all uprights provided with base plates or prevented some other way from slipping or sinking?
3. Have any uprights, ledgers, branches or struts been provided?
4. Is the scaffold is secured to the building in enough places to prevent collapse? Have any ties been removed since the scaffold been erected?
5. Are there sufficient boards' at all working platforms in use?

6. Are all boards free from obvious defects and are they arranged to avoid traps?
7. Are there warning notices to prohibit the use of any scaffold that is incomplete (e.g., not fully boarded)?
8. At every side where a person can fall more than 2 m are the platform gangways and runs provided with guardrails and toe-boards?
9. Who is responsible for the inspections; are they carried out and recorded?

Excavations

During an excavation on a site may be workers first and last job. If the sides collapse, there may be no escape. There is almost no ground which will not collapse under certain conditions. If there is any doubt what so ever about the safety of the sides, they should be timbered or battened. Timbering materials should always be provided on site.

Check Points

1. Is the excavation more than 1.2 m deep?
2. Is the timber provided strong enough to support the sides of the excavation?
3. Is the method of putting in timbering a safe one?
4. Is the angle of batter appropriate?
5. Are the excavation inspected daily, and the timbering weekly?
6. Is there safe access to the excavation?
7. Is there a barrier to prevent people falling in?
8. Is the stability of the excavation being affected by vehicles which come too near?
9. If vehicle tip into an excavation, are the properly secured stop blocks provided?

Road Work

Check Points

1. If the work being done on a sloping roof of more than 30 degrees, or less than 30, but which is slippery? If so are there crawling ladders or crawling boards? Are these being used? If crawling boards or ladders are not provided does the roof structure itself provide a safe hand hold and foot hold?
2. For sloping roofs or work near the edge of flat roofs, is there sufficient edge protection to prevent falls of materials and people?
3. Is any one working on or near fragile materials such as asbestos, cement sheets or glass? If so are crawling boards provided and used and warning notices posted?
4. Have all roof lights been properly covered or provide with barriers?
5. During sheeting operations are precautions taken to prevent people falling from the edge of the sheet?
6. Where others are working under roof work, are precautions taken to prevent debris falling unto them?

Machinery

Some dangerous parts like gears, chain drives, and rotating shafts with projecting keys and set screws are easy to recognize. Others are not so obvious, like projecting engine shafts.

Check Points

1. Are there any dangerous parts?
2. Are they guarded?
3. Is the guard secured and in good repair?

Hoists

A platform hoist must be protected by a substantial enclosure and the enclosure must be fitted with gates where access is needed. A platform hoist can be dangerous if the gates are not kept shut. Hoists are required to be inspected weekly and thoroughly examined every six months by a competent person.

Check Points

1. Who is responsible for these inspections, are they carried out and recorded?
2. Is there an enclosure, where it is necessary to prevent people being struck by any moving part of platform or the hoist or materials in it?
3. Are gates provided at all gates?
4. Are the gates kept shut except when the platform is at landing?
5. Is the control rope so arranged that the hoist can be operated from one position only?
6. Is the safe working load clearly marked on the hoist?
7. Is there a proper signaling system?
8. If the hoist is for materials only, is there a notice on the platform or cage prohibiting people from riding on it? Is this notice obeyed?

Electricity

The main causes of electrical accidents on sites are from electrical equipment or lighting from overhead electric power lines and from underground cables. Treat all electrical equipment with respect.

Check Points

1. Signs of damage to apparatus especially portable equipment.

2. Signs of damage to other coverings of wires and cables.
3. Are all connections to power points by proper plugs, etc. and not bare ends of cables?
4. Are there signs of interference with equipment, damaged or otherwise?
5. Are there any overhead electric lines? If so, is there anything (a crane, forklift truck, tipper lorry, excavator or scaffolding) which might touch these lines? If so, has the electricity supply to these lines been cut off?
6. If not, what other precautions have been taken?
7. If there is an electric underground cable near the work being carried out, is the line of the cable known, has it been located and marked and have precautions been taken to prevent contact?

❐ ❐ ❐

CHAPTER 4

Tables Used for Systematic Construction Safety

Table 1:	Unsafe Conditions and Acts During and After Project Construction
Table 2:	Various Stores at Construction Site
Table 3:	Safety Implementation Record
Table 4:	Plan for Safety Inspections
Table 5:	Handing and Taking Over Steps in Construction Stages

Table 1: Unsafe Conditions and Acts During and After Project Construction

Sl. No.	Accidents	Receiving and storage	Civil work	Instal-lation	Testing and commissioning	Operation	Main-tenance
1.	Accidents due to pit falls in trench excavation		**	*			
2.	Fall of persons from height		**	**			
3.	Accidents due to failure of cranes, slings, ropes, D shackles	**		**			
4.	Fires	**		*	**	*	
5.	Falling of objects on human body		*	*			
6.	Road accidents	**	*	*			
7.	Collapse of structures, walls and slabs		**	*			
8.	Electric shocks		*	*	**		**
9.	Explosions and fires				**	**	

Cont...

10.	Equipment failures				**	**	
11.	Lightening strokes		*	*		*	
12.	Flashovers				**	**	
13.	Unsafe equipment					**	

* Old, inadequate rating, prone to failure.

Table 2: Various Stores at Construction Site

Sl. No.	Category	Title of the stores	Temporary	Permanent	Remarks
1.	Civil	• Cement store • Steel stores • Tool and tackle store • Structure store • Other stores for construction items	* * * * *	 *	
2.	Equipment stores	• Indoor stores • Outdoor stores	* *	* *	

Cont...

3.	Inflammable material stores	• Paint store • Fuel store • Chemical stores		* * *	
4.	Consumable stores	• Outdoor stores • Indoor stores	* *	* *	
5.	Spare parts	• Indoor spares stores (Mechanical) • Indoor spares stores (Electrical) • Indoor stores • Others		* * *	
6.	Vehicle and transport stores and Material handling stores	• Indoor stores for vehicle spares		*	

Table 3: Safety Implementation Record

(To be submitted by the Contractor at the beginning of each month)

Contractor:

For the month of :

Sl. No.	Activity	Date	Remarks
1.	**Safety training** • Induction training • Refresher training • Pre-job training • Others		Total number of persons attended
2.	**Safety inspection** • Excavation • Form work • Hoist • Electrical • Ladder • Hot work • House keeping • Plant and equipment • Scaffolding • Storage of materials		Monthly frequency
3.	**Safety meeting** • Site meeting • Committee meeting		Mention main agenda/focus
4.	**Safety promotion** • Safety signage's • Safety posters		Mention the number displayed
5.	**Safety campaign** • Safety skills • Safety celebrations		To be conducted regularly

Sign of Safety Officer **Sign of Site-In charge**

Table 4: Plan for Safety Inspections

Sl. No.	Type of Inspection	Frequency	Inspected by Contractor	Inspected by Safety Officer
1.	PPE	Weekly	Safety engineering and site in-charge	Random
2.	Excavation	Weekly	Civil/Strul., safety engg. and site incharge	Random
3.	Lifting tool and tackles (Chain pulley blocks, slings and D-shackles etc.)	Weekly	Mech. engg., safety engg. and site incharge	Random
4.	Crane and Hoist	Weekly	Mech. engg., safety engg. and site incharge	Random
5.	Electrical installation and connection	Weekly, All new connection and modification	Elect. engg., safety engg., site incharge	Random
6.	Ladder	Weekly	Civil and strl. engg. safety engg. and site incharge	Random
7.	Hot work	Daily	Safety engg. and site incharge	Random

Cont...

Sl. No.	Type of Inspection	Frequency	Inspected by Contractor	Inspected by Safety Officer
8.	Compressed gas cylinder	Weekly	Safety engg., store incharge	Random
9.	House keeping	Daily	Safety engg. and site incharge	Random
10.	Plant and equipment	Weekly	Mech. engg., safety engg. and site incharge	Random
11.	Construction equipment	Fortnightly and First use	Mech engg., safety engg. and site incharge	Random
12.	Fire protection	Fortnightly	Safety and fire engg. and site incharge	Random
13.	Scaffolding, staging and Form work	Weekly and All new and modification	Civil and strl. engg. safety engg. and site incharge	Random
14.	Man basket	Weekly	Mech./safety engg. site Incharge	Random
15.	Storage material	Weekly	Store and site incharge, safety engg.	Random

Contractor must submit the schedule of each inspection mentioning the date and time for each month, to the Authorities, within 3 days of each calendar month.

All inspections must be carried out as per the checklist.

Stage Wise Internal Handing Over Procedure

During the project construction period, the total activities are divided into distinct major stages and procedure for handing over from one stage to the next stage is defined. For this the table given below is used.

Table 5: Handing and Taking Over Steps in Construction Stages

Construction stages	Pre condition for starting	Handing over/taking over
1. Receiving and storage	– Roads ready – Site office opened – Stores ready	– By transporters to store keeper
2. Civil works	– Soil investigations and civil designs completed – Construction water, power arranged – Subcontracts finalized – Construction materials arranged	– Manager civil takes – over the site and begins civil works
3. Erection work (zone wise)	– Completion of the civil work in the zone	– Manager civil to manager erection
4. Equipment testing and test of subsystems (zone wise)	– Completion of erection work in the zone – Auxiliary ready	– Manager erection to manager testing

5. Commissioning tests	– Completion of equipment tests, subsystem tests – Auxiliary power available. – Loads available.	– Manager Testing to Manager Commissioning or: one manager for testing/ commissioning
6. System Engineering and performance tests	– Completion of commissioning tests in every zone – Associated transmission lines/loads/ generating stations available	– Jointly by manager – Commissioning, plant owner and concerned Transmission/ generating agency under responsibility of manager commissioning

The safety responsibilities are owned by each and every group under the leadership of concerned group manager and total site manager.

Internal handing over document is signed by the handing over manager and taking over manager.

❐ ❐ ❐

CHAPTER 5

Use of Checklists to Ensure Construction Safety

Construction Safety Checklists were made with the idea of making construction work much safer. These checklists prove very useful when wanting to verify whether a construction site is fitted to do construction work according to construction safety regulations. Less chances of repeat accidents or disasters as you progress along construction jobs is what you would want and these checklists greatly help make this possible.

Given all this, it is good practice to build a Construction Safety Checklist and continually add on to this as a principal contractor gets to identify more potential hazards to look out for in construction work.

One might wonder what it is that would most usually comprise a Construction Safety Checklist, so to satisfy that curiosity, below is a list of the essential things that are to be included in a Construction Safety Checklist:

- **Site inspections**

  Walk around the site and check for any small structure present on the site that was not included in the plans and may need to be demolished, a depression that could possibly indicate the presence of something that has been buried in site or this may even lead to discovery of an underground tank. You may also consider hiring an independent contractor to do the site inspections.

- **Employee site orientation**

  Prior to starting construction work, the workers must be made aware of the unique risks and hazards present in the site. Knowing what to look out for in the site would greatly help avert disasters.

- **Worksite fenced off**

  Placing a fence around the site would keep away outsiders from getting in and exposing themselves to the potential dangers in the construction site. Also, these trespassers may end up taking equipment or materials needed for the site. The fence would prove a good obstacle that would be a challenge to get through.

- **Protective equipment**

  After having assessed the risks in the site, the principal contractor must make sure that all protective equipment has been provided and that all workers are properly making use of such equipment.

- **First aid**

  Make sure that there is sufficient first aid equipment and facilities are made available and easily accessible in the construction site. First aid must be quick in response and done in a proper manner.

- **Construction signs**

Placement of construction signs around the parameters of the site to keep the general public a good distance from the site would do well to ensure their safety.

- **Construction tools and equipment**

Testing tools and equipment to verify that they are working properly is another measure that needs to be taken just before construction work starts. This must also be applied to all electrical leads or outlets. The list above is merely something to start off with and build up on. Construction Safety Checklists could include many more things. This may very well prove to be a good starter.

The checklist contains itemized problems and failures. The items on the list may or may not apply to the entire situation and only acts as a reminder to stimulate thought process Checklist approach can be used at various stages of project implementation. Many standards have standardized the hazard identification checklists. Here are some examples which are not an exhaustive one and may be suitably modified as per requirement.

Plant Hazard Identification Checklist

Sl. No.	Elements/Items of Checklist	Yes/No	Further Information
1.	**Layout of the Plant** • Is area properly demarcated? • Is aisles provided? • Are there areas for emergency vehicles? • Do demarcated storages for raw materials and products exist? • Are there safe clearances from overhead electrical lines? • Are the interdistances between units and between equipment adequate? • Is there adequate platforms and railings wherever required for safe working?		
2.	**Safe Operating Procedures** • Are written procedures available for all critical operations? • Are employee and contractors' workers made aware of these procedures? • Are procedures available for handling hazardous chemicals? • Are MSDS available for all hazardous chemicals? • Are hazardous chemicals stored as required?		
3.	**House Keeping** • Are the floors, staircases and aisles clean and free from obstructions? • Is there any oil/chemical spillage in the work areas? • Are all tools and accessories kept in their designated place? • Is there any accumulation of dry grasses in and around work space?		

4.	**Personal Protective Equipment (PPE)** • Are there adequate PPE's available to various activities, available? • Are employees and contractor' workers adequately trained to use PPE"s? • Is there proper storage of PPE's? • Are the PPE's maintained? • Are there adequate replacements available?		

(MSDS stands for Material Safety Data Sheet)

Everyday some one responsible may identify all the enlisted hazards as per checklist and further it must be discussed in daily project meetings headed by the project head.

Name and Designation of the Person WHO inspected:

Date and Time of Inspection:

Initials of the Inspector:

Checklist for Lifting Hoist

Sl. No.	Particulars	Observation	Remark
1.	**Type of Hoist**		
2.	**State the following hoist particulars** • Manufacturer • Model No. • Safe load carrying capacity		
3.	**Mast Base** • Is the base founded upon the ground or ground bearing slab and has this been correctly prepared for hoist loads? • Is the base founded upon a suspended floor slab or deck and have structured props been provided below the hoist mast? • Does a scaffold or structure steel gantry support the base and is layout designed to withstand impact buffer loads?		
4.	**Mast Ties** • Have fixings into brick work been tested? • Are all nuts and bolts within the tie arm assemblies tightened to the correct torque and of a self locking type? • Where tie-arms are fixed to main structural beams, are the bottom flanges of these beams adequately restrained? • Where tie-arms are of a length in excess of four meters is a support against the self weight of the tie-arm required and if so, has the tie been fitted?		

The checklist has been completed in respect of the work and equipment identified.

Name: **Sign.** **Designation** **Date**

Checklist for Excavations

Sl. No.	Particulars	Observation	Remark
1.	Have any previous inspection and/or audits of excavation been carried out? Have all major findings been corrected?		
2.	**Present conditions** • Is an adequate supply of shoring material (timber, trench sheets, props or other supporting materials) made available before excavation work begins? • Does the excavation have safe access and egress? • Is a safe shoring method used for support? • Does competent person depending on the stature of the soil suggest slopes of the excavation? • Is the excavated material stacked/dumped away from the edge of the excavation (minimum 2 meters away)? • Is the excavated edge is free from loose material, etc.? • Does the excavation have proper barrication? • Does the barrication signage's visible at night? • Is any dumping yard/space specified for excess excavated materials? • Is any underground service, e.g., water pipeline, underground electrical lines, telephone lines etc. exist? If yes, what is the precautionary measures to prevent the damage? • Is the area free from poisonous flora and fauna?		

Cont...

Sl. No.	Particulars	Observation	Remark
	• Is the side walls are free from the crack line? • Is any banks man provided to guide the drivers of dump trucks? Is he well aware of his responsibilities? • Are the dump trucks parked far away from the edges of the side walls? • Is there adequate safety signboards displayed in local and English languages? • Is sufficient illumination available at all around the excavated area? • Is the work being carried out through a valid permit to work system? • Has the equipment certified for the job? Has the Operators certified to operate the equipments? • Are the swinging areas of the moving equipments free from any obstructions? • Is the excavated area checked regularly and after every spell of rain or storm by the competent fellow? • Are necessary PPE's provided to all workmen and they using it meticulously?		

The checklist has been completed in respect of the work and equipment identified.

Name: **Sign.** **Designation** **Date**

Crane Inspection Checklist

Sl. No.	Description	Observation Yes/No	Remark
1.	Is the crane inspected previously and the no shortfall as mentioned in the previous inspection is left unattended?		
2.	Does the crane have a valid third party competent authority's test certificate?		
3.	Has the crane gone through major changes/alteration etc. by which the stability/integrity of the crane in doubt?		
4.	Is the condition of the boom members O.K.?		
5.	Is the hoist chain or hoist rope free of kinks or twists and not wrapped around the load?		
6.	Has it been ensured that no less than 3 wraps of rope remain on the drum when the hook is in the extreme low position?		
7.	Is the reeling of rope drum free from overlaps?		
8.	Has the brakes been tested?		
9.	Does the lifting hook has a safety latch that will prevent the rope from slipping out?		
10.	Is there a load over hoist limit switch which will prevent lifting rope failure due to over hoisting?		
11.	Is there a boom back stop alarm and cut-off devices installed which will protect the crane boom from exceeding safe limit of hoisting? (in crawler cranes)		
12.	Is there a load chart available in the crane?		

Cont...

Sl. No.	Description	Observation Yes/No	Remark
13.	Is there a boom angle indicator installed and clearly visible from the operator's cabin? (only for mechanical cranes)		
14.	A load moment indicator (LMI) (an onboard computer) installed and is functional? (available only on hydraulic cranes)		
15.	Is the tyre pressure and condition (for tyre mounted cranes) or crawlers (for crawler cranes) O.K.?		
16.	Is the condition of the outriggers O.K.? Check for any oil leakage from the outrigger hydraulic system visually)?		
17.	Have correctly sized outrigger pads with appropriate wood or other bearers been supplied?		
18.	Is the condition of the boom, lattice or telescopic, acceptable? Check for distortion damages.		
19.	Is a 5 kg. DCP fire extinguisher available at operator's cabin?		
20.	Is the crane operator is competent and medically fit and has been certified the eye sight by ophthalmologist for work?		
21.	Has the crane operator been instructed that no sudden acceleration/de-acceleration is permitted during the moving of the load?		
22.	Has the crane operator been instructed not to move loads over people?		
23.	Has the crane operator been instructed not to leave the load suspended?		

Height Work Permit/Checklist

(For working at height above 2 meter from ground height)

Sl. No.	Checklist	Observation		Remarks	Name of the workmen deployed at site	Designation
1.	Height of working	from – to – mtrs				
2.	Safety helmet and shoes	Reqd.	Not reqd.			
3.	Condition of full body harness	Good	Bad			
4.	Whether fall arresters are used	Yes	No			
5.	Mention the number of fall arresters being used	Nos.				
6.	Full body harness properly tied or not	Yes	No			
7.	Scaffolding	Reqd.	Not reqd.			
8.	Whether steel scaffolding material used	Yes	No			
9.	All openings and end of the platforms located 2 m or more be covered from fall of persons or materials.	Done	Not reqd.			

Cont...

Sl. No.	Checklist	Observation		Remarks	Name of the workmen deployed at site	Designation
10.	Condition and arrangement of scaffolding for working at height.	Saisfactory	Not satisfact			
11.	In case of using ladder, check the strength and position.	Done	N/A			
12.	All electrical equipment are grounded.	Yes	N/A			
13.	Adequate illumination for height working.	Yes	N/A			
14.	Whether warning signs and barrication is installed.	Yes	N/A			
15.	Whether all lifting tackles/cranes are tested by competent authority.	Yes	N/A			
16.	Whether vertical lifeline placed near ladder.	Yes	No			
17.	Whether horizontal lifeline provided at work place.	Yes	No			
18.	Whether proper man-basket are being used.	Yes	No			

Checklist for Temporary Electrical Connections

Sl. No.	Particulars	Observations	Remark
1.	Have any previous inspection and/or audits of temporary electrical connections being carried out? Have all major findings been rectified?		
2.	Where mains voltage has to be used are trip devices, e.g., earth leakage circuit breakers (ELCBs): (a) provided (inspection record) (b) used?		
3.	Are ELCBs: (a) externally protected from adverse weather. (b) Protected from damage, dust and dampness (c) checked daily by users?		
4.	Are cables and leads protected from damage by (a) protective enclosure (conduit) (b) positioning?		
5.	Are all connections to the system: (a) properly made and (b) are suitable plugs used?		
6.	Are spare holes/openings of power panels closed?		
7.	Is IR (Insulation Resistance) value checked and recorded?		
8.	Are earth connections to DB tightened and all switches checked?		
9.	Are all flexible cables and cable joints placed 3 m above the ground level?		
10.	Have all electrical operated equipments ear-thed properly?		
11.	Are only 3 core double insulated flexible wires used for power connection to lighting fixtures?		

Cont...

Sl. No.	Particulars	Observations	Remark
12.	Are all flood lights covered with protective glasses?		
13.	Is all lighting fixtures fixed on rigid frames?		
14.	Are all power panels, DBs, power points protected from weather?		
15.	Is the electrical room locked and is the key is readily available with the designated electrician?		
16.	Are 'Danger' sign displayed at required locations?		
17.	Are all DBs and electrical panels located in easily accessible area?		

The checklist has been completed in respect of the work (contractor).

Name: **Sign.** **Designation** **Date**

Checklist for Ladder

Sl. No.	Particulars	Observations	Remark
1	Have any previous inspection and/or audits of ladder been carried out? If so have all the major findings been rectified?		
2.	Are ladders: (a) The right means of access for the job? (b) In good condition? (c) Secured to prevent them slipping onwards or sideways?		
3.	Do ladder rise 1 m above their landing place? If not, is other handhold available?		
4.	Are the ladder positioned so that users: (a) Don't have obstruct (b) Climb over obstacles?		
5.	Do ladders rest against a solid surface and not on fragile or insecure materials?		
6.	Are ladders spliced in make-shift arrangement?		
7.	On step ladders: (a) Are the stays, chains or cords in good condition? (b) Is the ladder placed sufficiently near the work on a firm level surface?		
8.	Are ladders: (a) Positioned clear of overhead electric cables? If not. (b) Has the power supply been isolated? (c) Secured at one end to prevent them slipping outwards?		

The checklist been completed in respect of the work (contractor).

Name: **Signature** **Designation** **Date**

Checklist for House Keeping

Sl. No.	Particulars	Observations	Remark
1.	Have any previous inspection and/or audits of house keeping been carried out? If so, have all the findings been rectified?		
2.	Are accesses and egresses to and from the work place kept clear and clean at all times?		
3.	Are there any tripping/slipping hazards? Are they reported and rectified quickly?		
4.	Are drains blocked or poor drainage (soft ground heavy underfoot). Is anything done to help this situation?		
5.	Are sufficient skips, bins located at all work area? Are the waste materials shifted to designated dump yard on daily basis?		
6.	Is material stored orderly and not causing obstruction/hazards?		
7.	Is the worksite cleaned and kept tidy and if work is suspended is the site cleaned and made safe before moving on go to another area?		
8.	Are the store, workshop, canteen, toilets, and rest shelters inspected and cleaned on regular basis?		
9.	Is the inside/outside of vehicle/plant inspected to ensure that they are maintained cleaned and tidy condition?		
10.	What is the method for handling of hazardous chemicals? Are the jutes; cottons; etc., used for cleaning of oily substances, to be dumped in designated area?		

11.	How the medical waste generated in first-aid center, e.g., used gauge, bandage, cottons are kept? Are these destroyed with proper care to prevent the chances of infection?		
12.	Are all flammable materials kept in proper way? Is safety signage displayed to aware the workmen?		
13.	Is the designated house keeping gang members trained in 5S system?		

The checklist has been completed in all respect of the work (contractor).

Name: **Signature** **Designation** **Date**

Checklist for Plant and Equipment

Sl. No.	Particulars	Observations	Remark
1.	Have any previous inspection and/or audits on plant and equipments been carried out? Have all major findings been complied with?		
2.	Is right plant and machinery being used for the job?		
3.	Are all dangerous part guarded? (e.g., exposed gears, chain drives, projecting engine shafts etc.)		
4.	Are guards: • Secured. • In good repair. • If modified, is it certified by a competent person?		
5.	Is the machinery: • Maintained, and • Are all safety device operating correctly?		
6.	Are all the operators trained and competent? e.g., do the plant operators hold a valid license for which they are operating?		
7.	Where locked system is fitted do they work and are they regularly maintained?		
8.	Is the plant checked when first arriving on site?		
9.	Are daily checking and recordings carried out?		
10.	Are unauthorized uses are prohibited?		

11.	Does the assessment identify areas and parts of the plants, which require being inspected either weekly or daily?		
12.	Are the results of the inspection and examination recorded, including any faults or defects found?		
13.	Has the plant a current test certificate and is it held with the plant?		
14.	Are the certificates for any lifting equipment carried with the plant available, e.g., shackles, slings etc.?		

The checklist has been completed in respect of the work (Contractor).

Name: **Signature** **Designation** **Date**

Checklist for Fire Prevention

Sl. No.	Particulars	Observations	Remark
1.	What are the major electrical equipments at the site?		
2.	What are the precautions taken against transformer fires?		
3.	What is the lightening protection at the site and at the flammable storage area?		
4.	What are the major fire risk activities/jobs carried out at the site?		
5.	What are the control measures for such fire risks?		
6.	What are the major flammable storage at the site?		
7.	What are the fire protection measures in flammable storage area?		
8.	What are the protection against spillage and consequent fire?		
9.	Who is responsible for house keeping at the flammable storage area?		
10.	What are the other significant fire risk areas in the site?		
11.	What are the major control measures for such fire risks?		
12.	Who is responsible for inspection and maintenance of fire protection systems?		
13.	Are the records of inspection and maintenance kept?		
14.	How the fire protection measures are communicated to the people at the site?		

15.	How the special fire risk areas at the site are identified, demarked and communicated to all people at the site? (cautionary signs, signals and caution boards)		
16.	Is mock drill conducted? What are the frequencies?		
17.	How many persons at the site are trained in fire fighting?		

The checklist has been completed in respect of the work (Contractor).

Name: **Signature** **Designation** **Date**

Checklist for Scaffolding/Staging/Formwork

Sl. No.	Particulars	Observations	Remark
1.	Have any previous inspection and/or audits of scaffolding been carried out? Have all major findings been corrected?		
2.	Working platforms (inclusive of walkways) and guard rails, toe guards, knee guards etc.? (a) Are the working platforms of adequate width? (b) Are the overhangs of planks between 300-500 mm and overlaps of planks between 600-800 mm? (c) Are the planks properly supported and secured? (d) Are top guardrails and intermediate guardrails provided and properly secured along the open edges of the platform?		
3.	Access/egress (a) Are the ladders provided for access properly secured? (b) With the top end at least 1 m above the platform? Better restrict the ladders to 4 m length. (c) Are the ladders made of Aluminium/steel?		
4.	Rigidity and stability of the staging (a) Is the staging resting on firm and solid ground with the fittings properly tightened. (b) Is the framework sufficiently reinforced and immobilized? (c) Are scaffolds and working platforms securely fastened to the building/structure and braces or guyed properly?		

	(d) Whether the scaffold is secured to the building/fixed structure to prevent collapse of scaffolding?		
5.	Miscellaneous (a) Are platforms, ladders and walkways free from obstructions? (b) Are wire ropes, used for suspending the hanging secured properly? (c) Is the diameter of tubular scaffold is more than 48 mm and wall thickness more than 2-3 mm? (d) Are wooden planks free from cracks and more than 35 mm thick and sound? (e) Are loose materials, electric wires and other parts left on staging? (f) Are electrical wiring properly insulated/without joints and safe? (g) Is sufficient and proper lighting provided for staging in dark areas and for night working? (h) Whether scaffolds are mounted on proper base plates to prevent slipping or sinking? (i) Are the planks and other staging materials in good condition? (j) Whether the couplers are causing deformation in tubes? (Couplers should be made of drop-forged forged steel or equivalent material)		

- Separate certificate to be prepared for every staging, grouping of several staging is not allowed.
- Only persons trained and with skills in staging/scaffolding only to be allowed to erect supervise staging work.
- Every scaffold should be constructed, erected and maintained so as to prevent collapse or accidental displacement when in use. Hence, scaffolding should be erected, altered, or dismantled by only competent person under supervision.

After erection, scaffold should be inspected at least once in a week and a written report of inspection is to be kept.

This is to certify that the above staging is suitable and safe for men to work on.

Name and signature of Site Engineer (Contractor):

Date of Issue:

Checklist for Material Storage

Sl. No.	Particulars	Observations	Remark
1.	To avoid fire hazards, smoking and open fires are strictly prohibited near timber yard.		
2.	To stack separately: (a) Wooden slippers. (b) Runners. (c) Ballies. (d) Plywoods. (e) Bamboos.		
3.	To check whether stacking of following items of different sizes are stacked separately in steel yard with enough space all around: (a) Steel reinforcement. (b) M.S. joints (c) Angles. (d) Channels. (e) Flats. (f) M.S. pipes.		
4.	The steel items to be stacked over wooden slippers or raised platforms – but not on ground.		
5.	Adequate fire fighting arrangements provided at each storage place.		
6.	Do all workers use PPE's? Do all fellows are trained for manual material handling?		
7.	Are chemicals stored separately? Have they tagged properly? Is MSDS of all hazardous chemicals available at store?		

8.	Are all flammable materials stored separately? Is 'No Smoking' Board displayed? Is there adequate ventilation system?		
9.	Has all full and empty cylinders kept separately? Are they tagged properly? Is 'No Smoking' Board displayed? Is all acetylene cylinders are kept in upright condition?		

The checklist has been completed in all respect of the work identified.

Name: Signature Designation Date

Verified by company executive:

Name: Signature Designation Date

Chain Pulley Block Inspection Checklist

Parameters of Inspection	Yes	No
Is the load test certificate available for the particular equipment?		
Is the Tag with SWL and Sl.No. Imprinted fixed on the chain pulley block?		
External Features		
Physical condition of the outer cell, whether corroded, rusted, cracked etc. OK?		
Condition of the load chain O.K.? (Check each link of the chain)		
Are they free from rust?		
Is the device free from cracks, depression, signs of weakening, kinks, distortion? (The chain is rejected even a single link is damaged)		
Check the Gears		
Condition of the operating chain O.K.?		
Condition of the lifting hook O.K.?		
Are secured means of hook in O.K. condition?		
Is the throat opening O.K.? (Reject if distortion causing an increase in throat opening exceeds 15 percent)		
Free from any signs of wear or rusting? (Reject if any wear exceeding 10 percent of the original section dimension of the hook or its load pin)		
Free from any deformation? (Reject if any bending or twisting exceeded 10 degrees from the plane of the unbent hook)		
Free from cracks, depression, signs of weakening?		
Is the hook safety latch available and is in opening condition?		
Is the suspension hook/lug in good condition?		

Are all the split pins for all locking pin/nut bolt in place?		
Internal features (remove the outer cover but do not dismantle the components inside)		
Physical condition of the inner shell, free from corrosion, rust, crack, etc.?		
Check the gears: – Are they placed well in their original position? – Are the gears physically in good condition? – Are the bearings, pins, rollers in good condition?		
Is the operation chain wheel O.K.?		
Load sprocket, idle sprocket, in acceptable condition?		
Are the CAM/Ratchet in good repair? (Do not dismantle the same)		
Are the nuts, bolts are properly placed and fits well in place?		

Inspected by: **Signature:** **Date:**

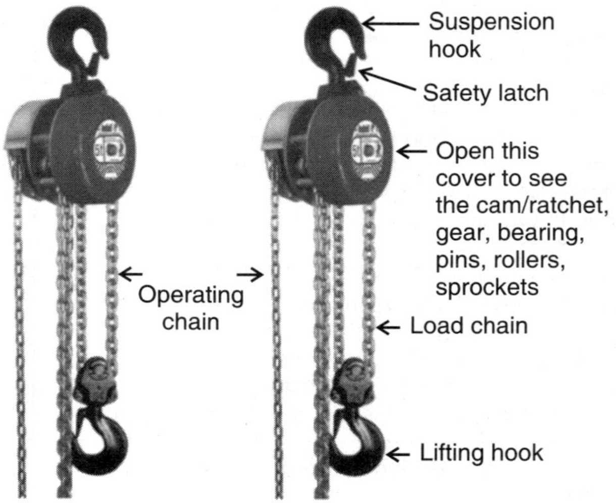

Fig. 5.1: ***Chain Pulley Block.***

Checklist for Compressed Gas Cylinders

Transporting and Moving Cylinders	Yes	No
Are valves closed when moving cylinders?		
Are cylinders secured in a cradle, sling board or pallet?		
Are cylinders kept in a vertical position?		
Before movement are regulators removed, and caps securely placed over valves?		
Placing Cylinders		
Are cylinders kept in an upright position?		
Are cylinders placed where they will not become part of an electrical circuit or come in contact with piping or layout tables used for grounding?		
When in use are cylinders secured to prevent knocking them over?		
Are cylinders placed where they will not be exposed to flames or heat sources?		
Are cylinders with O_2 and or flammable gases prevented from being placed in a confined area?		
Storing Cylinders		
Are O_2 cylinders kept separated from fuel gas cylinders and combustible materials by at least 20 feet?		
Are cylinder valve closed and capped when empty?		
Are separated empty and full cylinders marked as such?		
Are 'No Smoking' signs posted in storage areas?		
Are cylinder contents marked?		
When storage racks are used is an adequate floor provided?		
Are cylinders, valves and apparatuses free from oily or greasy substances?		

Are storage area away from heat sources?		
Using Cylinders		
Are proper handling techniques applied while cylinders are used?		
Do craftsmen stand to the side when connecting regulators, slowly open and immediately close?		
Do safety devices show evidences of abuse or misuse?		
Are defective valves, leaky cylinders reported and replaced?		
Are flashback arrestors used on oxygen and acetylene cylinder connection hoses?		
Are proper color hose pipes used in the cylinders?		

The checklist has been completed in respect of the work identified.

Checked by (contractor)

Name: **Signature:**

Checklist for Hot Work, Cutting and Welding

Hot work	**Yes**	**No**
Does contractor has a written procedure for hot work?		
Does the procedure identify the competent person?		
Is the written procedure followed as observed by field tours?		
Cutting and Welding		
Are welding and cutting operation continuously monitored?		
Are fire extinguishers maintained in the immediate area?		
Are fire blankets used to protect from sparks, slag or hot places of metal?		
Are welding screens used to protect workers in the area from flash burns?		
Are torches removed from confined spaces when not in use?		
Are stand by fire watchers used?		
Are O_2 and DA cylinders provided with proper valve guards and labels?		
Is trolley in good condition and wheel with minimum 400 mm dia, available with chains for shifting gas cylinders?		
Is contractor well equipped for proper storage of spare cylinders (chains, separate storage of DA, LPG, O_2 and Ar, flammables etc.) and follows best practices?		
Is the gas cutting torch of reputed make, ISI marked, installed with non return valve and flash back arrestor at both ends?		
Is the regulator designed double stage and with two gauges?		
Are regulator pressure gauge in working condition, visible and not damaged?		
Are all cylinders in use provided with separate keys placed on cylinder valves?		

Are the gas hoses in good condition without cuts and damages?		
Are the gas hoses fixed properly with hose clamps (no wire tying)?		
Is the hose color code is being followed (red for DA and black or blue for O_2)?		
Are DA cylinders installed with fusible plugs?		
Is the gas cutter competent enough for the job and equipped with all tools, e.g., needle bunch for cleaning carbon from hose orifice, spark lighters etc.?		
Is the welding machine body got separate grounding (at least 3.15 mm GI wire or flexible single core cable?		
Is that machine got switch/control or power off?		
Is the power supply cables double insulated?		
Is the primary cable is armored (preferred) connected through ELCB/RCCB of 30 mA sensitivity, joint free and provided with 3 pin, metal clad plug working or damage?		
Is the primary cable is adequate (minimum 4 sq. mm)?		
Is the primary cable connected to terminal which are enclosed and with no live part exposed?		
Is the primary cable connection completely insulated from with machine body?		
Is there any indication of burnt insulation of cable end because of over loading?		
Is secondary cable (welding and ear thing) are of adequate (minimum 50 square meter)?		
Is the welding machine, welding cable and ear thing cable got adequate length and joint free?		
Is the welding cable and ear thing cable are crimped with proper size lugs? (Hammering is not acceptable)?		

Is the welding holder marked IS and insulation not damaged?		
Is the welder competent enough and equipped with proper tools to be used, e.g., chipping tools, wire brush etc.?		
Is the welder helper is also equipped with all required PPEs including face shield, welding goggles, apron, safety boots etc.?		
Is ear thing cable got clamps with adjusting screws and is connected with crimped lug?		
Is the machine installed with voltage indicator/lamps?		
Is the control switches and regulators properly insulated?		
Is the control switches and regulators not damaged?		
Is the machine identified with label on its capacity and voltage?		
Is the welding machine connected with ELCB?		
Is the insulation resistance of machine measured and found to be more than at least 5 m-ohms?		

The checklist has been completed in respect of the work identified.

Checked by (Contractor)

Name: **Signature** **Designation** **Date**

Checklist for Man Baskets

Sl. No.	Particulars	Yes	No
1.	Are industry – accepted qualifications for crane operators used (including physical examinations)?		
2.	Are monthly inspections performed?		
3.	Are the annual crane inspection been performed?		
4.	Are equipment accidents investigated and reported?		
5.	Are suspended work baskets utilized by permission only?		
6.	Have basket designs been approved?		
7.	Is the basket properly labeled with load capacity?		
8.	Has a permit been utilized and documentation retained?		
9.	Is the operator certified and experienced for operating the equipment?		
10.	Are cranes maintained on a periodic basis and documentation available on site?		
11.	Has a crane arrival inspection report been completed for each crane?		
12.	Is the surface leveled and verified suitable for placement of crane?		
13.	Is the operator instructed not to leave the workplace with basket in suspended condition?		
14.	Is only medically fit personnel allowed to access in man basket?		
15.	Is secondary fall protection system exists?		

The checklist has been completed in respect of the work identified.

Checked by (Contractor)

Name: **Signature** **Designation** **Date**

Checklist for Personal Protective Equipment Requirements

Sl. No.	Particulars	Yes	No
1.	Are clothing requirements identified?		
2.	Are head and scalp protection provided in accordance with local requirements? • Are chin straps worn by all workmen? • Are hard hats and suspension systems maintained in a safe manner? • Are unsafe hard hats removed?		
	Eyes		
1.	Is eye protection required and worn in a proper manner?		
2.	Does eye protection meets IS requirements?		
3.	Are proper fitting side shields required and used?		
4.	Are face shields worn as required?		
5.	Are signs posted at bench grinders "Face shields required"?		
	Ears		
1.	Is hearing protection provided and used when required?		
2.	Have contractors identified areas where hearing protection is required?		
	Fingers, Hands and Wrists Have the contractors provided adequate hand protection and gloves designed to protect against specific hazards when required?		
	Toes, Feet and Legs		
1.	Are feet and toe protection provided and used as required?		
2.	Are hard-toed shoes worn when required?		
3.	Are shoes/boots worn substantial and adequate for the type of work performed?		

	Respiratory (Breathing)		
1.	Does the contractor have a program controlling: medical qualification, training, respirators?		
2.	Is fit testing conducted and documented?		
	Skin Are skin hazards identified and protection provided?		
	Back Does the contractor identify tasks where back injuries are common and encourage employees to use safe techniques?		

The checklist has been completed in respect of the work identified.

Checked by:

Name: **Signature** **Designation** **Date**

Checklist for Fire Prevention Actions

Sl. No.	Description and Desirable Features	Yes	No
1.	**Storage for inflammable materials** • Fire safety document issued or not? • Fire protection system in ready state or not? • Separate storage for each inflammable material or not? • Fire wall between store and other parts or not? • Good spark proof wiring or not? • No permission for smoking and flames or not? • Good house keeping maintained or not? • Safety audit conducted or not? • Security system intact or not? • Lighting protection or not? • Storage according to recommendations or not?		
2.	**Storage of equipment/spares** • Fire safety document issued or not? • Fire protection system in ready state or not? • Insurance coverage obtained and valid or not? • Good spark proof wiring used or not? • Separate store for transformer oil or not? • No permission for smoking and flames or not? • Good house keeping maintained or not? • Fire protection system O.K. or not? • Good security system intact or not? • Lighting protection given or not? • Storage according to recommendations or not?		
3.	**Civil works** • Fire safety document issued or not? • Fire protection system in ready state or not? • Good house keeping system maintained or not?		

	• Precautions taken while welding or not? • Good construction maintained or not? • Fire retardant materials are used or not? • Fire safety recommendations followed or not? • Good quality wiring used or not? • Compartmentation of rooms/ducts made or not? • Provisions of fire walls, fire escapes, fire hydrants, raw water systems, fire stations etc. are there or not?		
4.	**Installation work** • Fire safety document issued or not? • Fire protection system in ready state or not? • Welding is done with care or not? • No welding of oil filled tanks maintained or not? • No loose connection in temporary wiring checked or not? • Supervision during drying out of transformers is done? • Field quality checks for current carrying paths to ensure low resistance or not? • Field quality checks on gas filled and oil filled equipment, chemical piping for leakage joints checked or not? • Field quality checks on electrical clearances done or not? • Field quality checks on fire fighting systems done or not?		
5.	**Testing, commissioning work** • Fire safety document issued or not? • Fire protection system in ready state or not? • Field quality tests on equipments, protection systems, cooling systems are maintained or not? • Field quality tests on cooling systems are maintained?		

	• Field quality tests on fire fighting systems maintained? • Precautions while testing oil filled equipment maintained? Presence of fire engine. • Commission checks are done under close supervision? • Proper setting of relays or not? • Energizing under close observation or not?		
6.	**Operation** • Fire safety documents issued or not? • Fire protection system in ready state or not? • No overload beyond permissible limit maintained? • Supervision of temperature rise is done or not? • Supervise control boards carefully at regular intervals. Keep log book records. Inspect plant carefully at regular intervals. If any smoke? Any over heating? Any burning smell? Any abnormal sound? Any leakage? Any bearing overheating? • Attend to leakages, abnormal sounds, abnormal conditions promptly been done? • Follow safety rules for operations or not?		
7.	**Maintenance** • Document for maintenance of fire protection system is issued and followed or not? • Fire protection system in ready state or not? • Are they following planned inspection and periodic preventive maintenance and test plan? • Current carrying parts are inspected for tightness of joints, hardware and there are no burning or overheating marks? • Sharp corners are removed? • Any discoloration is investigated? • Insulators are cleaned? • Cooling system is maintained? • Transformer oil is maintained?		

	• Auxiliaries, protection systems, interlocks, battery systems, ventilation and air-conditioning systems are maintained? • Fire protection system is maintained? • Mock-drills of fire event for operation and maintenance are done regularly? • Maintenance of lighting systems, wiring, switchgears and protective systems are done? • Maintenance of switchgear and protective system is done?		

Any 'NO' is a major safety lapse and action must be initiated to set right immediately.

Checklist for Rigging Equipments

Sl. No.	Equipments	Yes	No
1.	**Rigging Equipment** • Does the contractor have an inspection program for rigging equipment? • Is there documentation by contractors for all rigging equipments? • Is defective rigging equipment tagged and removed from services? • Is rigging equipment protected from mud, dirt and chemical exposures? • Are rigging and lifting devices properly designed and installed for the task? • Are softeners used to protect from damage? • Are chain-falls and max-pullers prevented from being used as slings? • Are employees prevented from walking under loads? • Are containers covered and spillage prevented? • Is a competent person assigned to all rigging activities? • Are lifting beams stamped with the capacity of the beam?		
2.	**Wire Rope Slings** • Are SWL marked and Test Certificates available? • Is the sling stored properly? • Is it free from rusting, abrasion, cut marks, pressing, denting, bird caging, twist, kinks or core protrusion? • Is the sling free from wires broken or number of broken wires less than acceptable standard (i.e., < 6 wires in a lay or 3 wires in a strand)? • Is the sling diameter uniform throughout the length? (reject for > 10% or more reduction)		

	• Is the sling mechanically spliced? (hand spliced or wire rope clamps not allowed)		
3.	**Belt Sling** • Is the belt sling tested and certified and SWL marked conspicuously? • Is it free from exposure to corrosive, cuts, burn, and abrasion? • Free from any scratch, cut up to 1/10th of the belt with at any place? • All sewn joints intact and no where it is separated?		
4.	**DEE or BOW Shackes** • Is the tackle tested and certified and SWL marked on the body? • Free from any cracks, dent, distortion or weld mark, wear and tear? • Is the pin in good shape and not distorted. Not replaced with any other materials like nut and bolt etc.? • Are the eyes in a straight alignment and the threads in good condition?		

The Checklist has been completed in respect of the work identified.

Checked by (Contractor):

Name: **Signature** **Designation** **Date**

Flaws in a Wire Rope Sling

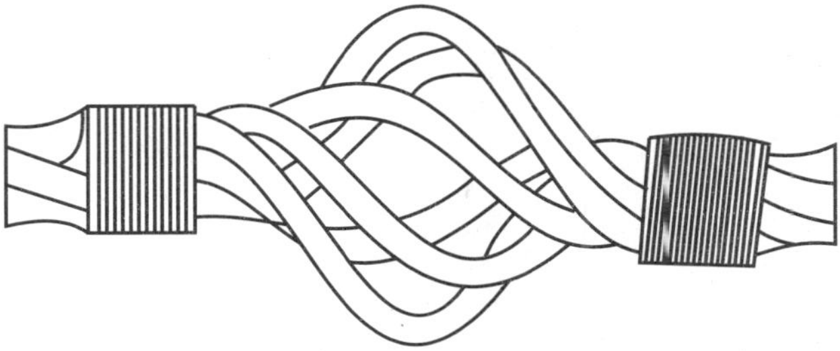

A "bird cage" caused by sudden release of tension and resultant rebound of rope from overload condition. These strands and wires will not return to their original positions.

Core protrusion as a result of torsional unbalance created by shock loading

Protrusion of IWRC resulting from shock loading

Replace rope if there are
- 5 or more broken wires in one Lay
- 3 or more broken wires in one strand in one Lay
- 3 or more broken wires in one Lay in Standing Ropes

In the UK, ropes must be replaced when there are more than 5% visible broken wires in any length of ten diameters.

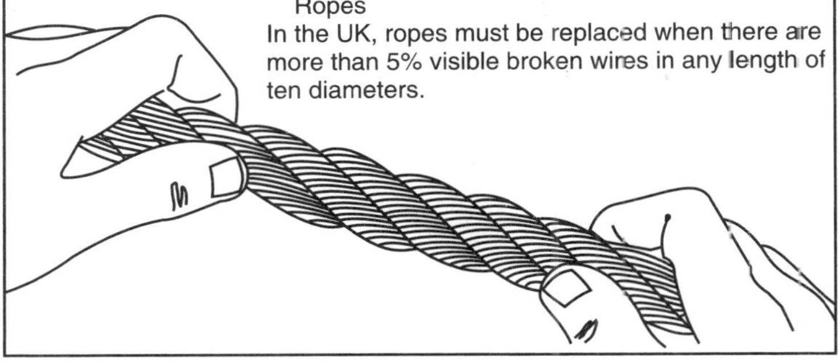

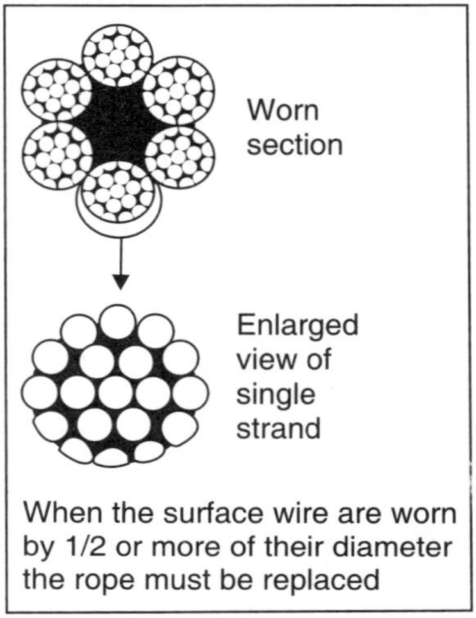

Flaws in a DEE Shackle

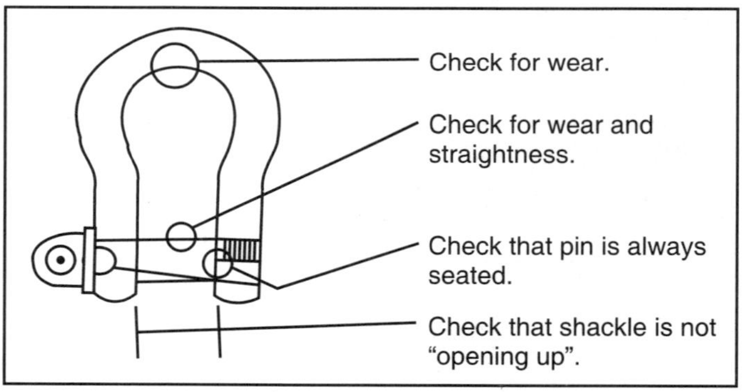

Vehicle Checklist

Date:

Name of contractor:

Vehicle identification number:

Sl. No.	Itmes	Condition Good/Bad	Function Good/Bad	Remarks
1.	Back/reverse alarms			
2.	Body and frame			
3.	Battery condition			
4.	Both side mirrors			
5.	Brakes			
6.	Clutch			
7.	Data name plate			
8.	Fire extinguisher			
9.	Fuel systems			
10.	Condition of glass			
11.	Horn			
12.	Lights			
13.	Hydraulic system			
14.	Parking brakes			
15.	Steering mechanism			
16.	Tracks, tyres, wheels			
17.	Turn signal indicator			
18.	Wind shield and wipers			
19.	Seat belts			
20.	Wheel chokes			

21.	Platform, ladder and hand rails (at corner)			
22.	Rotating part guarding of mixer power pack and fan blade			
23.	Condition of chute (pinch point/joints)			
24.	Precautionary message to avoid inserting the hand in the roller rotating the churner.			
25.	Driving license			
26.	RC/FC documents			
27.	Insurance documents			
28.	Any other site specific requirements.			

Acceptable/not acceptable with remarks if any:

Checked By: **Vehicle Driver:**

Checklist for Safety During Construction

Plant-------------------Zone-------------------Activity---------------

Check point	Cleared	Sign.	Date	Remark
Inspection of stores Store No. ...... Joint inspection of • Building • Flooring, walls, roof • Wiring • Passages • Roads • Any other point.				
Inspection of fire fighting facility • Water hydrants. • Water tanks and pumps, hoses. • Fire tenders. • Fire protection systems. • Portable extinguishers.				
Scaffolds, covers, ladders: • Covers for openings in slabs. • Vertical scaffolds. • Horizontal scaffolds. • Ladders. • Any other dangerous point.				
Inspection of civil works: • House keeping. • Isolation zone for passage of smoke. • Fence and gates. • Equipment foundations. • Cable trenches. • Roads.				

• Road cum rails. • Trench covers. • Building No. 1 • Building No. 2				
Inspection of structures: • Foundation. • Verticality. • Appearance. • Ear thing.				
Inspection of erected equipment: • Visual inspection. • Foundations. • Clearance. • Structure ear thing. • Terminal connections. • Site test report.				
Inspection of auxiliary system: • Auxiliary system No. 1 • Auxiliary system No. 2 • Auxiliary system No. 3				

❐ ❐ ❐

CHAPTER 6

Management of Safety in Construction Industry

INTRODUCTION

From project to construction, safety is more than just a legal requirement. The field of construction safety has undergone significant change over the past two decades. There are many reasons for this. Some of the prominent include the following:

- Technological changes that have introduced new hazards in construction sites.
- Proliferation of safety legislations.
- Increased pressure from assertive regulatory agencies.
- Realization by construction heads that a safe work place is the best work place.
- Skyrocketing safety and health care and workers compensation cost.

- Increased pressure from environmental groups and the public.
- A growing interest in ethics and corporate responsibility.
- Professionalization of construction safety occupations.
- Increased pressure from the labor organizations in general.
- Rapidly mounting costs associated with construction safety and other types of litigations.

All of these factors, when taken together, have made the construction safety management as more challenging and more important than it has ever been in the past. Safety management in construction industry consists of the following key elements:

- Visible management commitment to safety: the management of safety has been seen as an essential part of management's daily responsibilities, along with others such as quality, production, cost control, profitability and morale. Management can show commitment to safety by:
- Applying a high priority to safety in the planning and evaluation of all projects and constructions.
- Taking a personal interest in accidents, their investigations and follow up and in the welfare of the people concerned.
- Staffing safety department with experienced and competent personnel.
- Setting a good example.
- Management participation in safety inspections and safety meetings.
- Promoting safety in public, during company meetings and in publications.

- Always including safety instructions when issuing day to day instructions.
- Including safety as a priority item on the agenda at staff and management meetings.
- Safety should feature prominently in business plans and performance reports.
- It is managements' responsibility to ensure that all employees engaged in construction are properly equipped and trained and to motivate them so that all employees want to work safely.

To be successful in today's competitive world, managers must deliver results in time and within budget.

To Manage a Construction

- Understanding the basics.
- Planning a construction.
- Implementing a construction.
- Monitoring the performance is a must.

Defining a Construction

A construction is a series of activities designed to achieve a specific out come within a set budget and time scale.

What is a Construction?

- A project has clear starts and end points.
- A definite set of objectives.
- A sequence of activities in between.

Why to Use Construction Management?

- It gives more control.
- Provides proven tools and techniques.
- Help to lead team to reach objectives in time.

Identifying Key Features

- Defined start and end time.
- A planned approach.
- Organize resource.
- Synergy.
- Established goals.

Some Clarifications

- Some constructions are repetitive in nature; they are not processed as they have definite start and end points.
- A planned methodical approach is must to achieve expected result.
- An effective plan provides a template that guides the construction and work needs to be done.
- Some construction operates out side the normal routine business, others within – but all they require separate resources.
- Construction usually requires a team of people to get the job done. Construction team takes the responsibility for and gain satisfaction from their own objectives.
- Project construction offers new challenges and experiences.
- A construction offers result or creates something that did not exit previously.

Examining Key Roles

- A construction involves a wide range of people with very different skills and background.
- It is very important to understand and the parts that each of these key people plays.

WHO ARE THE KEY PLAYERS AND THEIR ROLES

Project Manager

- Responsible for achieving overall objectives and lead the project team.
- Produces detailed plan of action.
- Communicate the construction information to interested parties.
- Monitors progress to keep the construction on track.
- Motivates team members.

Key Team Member

- Assists project manager and provides knowledge if needed.
- Makes major contribution in examining the feasibility reports and planning.
- Lend technical support when needed.
- Is directly responsible for construction being completed on time.

Team Member

- Full time or part time man to carry out the action in the construction plan.
- Takes the responsibilities for completing the task set in construction plan.

Customers

- Internal and external customers who get the benefits from the changes brought about by the construction.
- Provides direction to project managers.
- Strongly influences the objectives of the project and how its success is meaningful.

Suppliers

- Provides materials, services needed to carry out the construction.
- Can be very supportive for the construction.
- Delivers goods, services on time and at a fixed price agreed at the out set of the construction.

Identifying the Essentials for Success

To achieve the desired out come of construction must have:

- Clear and defined goal.
- A committed team.
- A viable plan.
- Being flexible.

The Different Stages of a Construction

There are five stages of a construction:

- Initiation.
- Planning.
- Implementation.
- Monitoring.
- Closing.

Points to Remember

- Any new construction should be viewed as an existing opportunity to bring new skill and knowledge.
- There should be exchange of constructing suggestion.

Checking the Feasibility

Before we start any construction, we need to be certain that:

- Timing is right.
- Identifying the driving forces.
- Identifying the resisting forces.

- Driving forces: winning of last customers technological changes at customs.
- Resisting forces: people's resistance to change due to lack of information.

Prioritizing the Constructions

When managing number of constructions, we must evaluate which is most important in order to allocate time and resources.

- Seek opinion before prioritization.
- Scheduling of construction.
- Decide which construction offers the greatest potential value to the organization.
- Create master schedule to out line resource.

PRINCIPLES OF SAFETY MANAGEMENT

Safety management aims at eliminating unsafe acts and unsafe conditions by applying management techniques. The safety principles have been evolved during the twentieth century and are applicable universally.

Principle 1

Safety is an important management function of every organization (like production, maintenance, planning and construction).

The company management must have a written safety policy. Management must take up the responsibility of implementing the safety policy. Management is responsible for creating safety organization, set safety objectives, plan, monitor, and achieve desired results towards total safety.

Principle 2

Accidents are caused by unsafe acts and unsafe conditions.

Safety management is responsible for both. The unsafe acts and unsafe conditions are due to some lapse in safety management.

Principle 3

Behind one accident there are several chance misses.

The accident is a cumulating effect of multiple causes; one root cause and several contributory causes. For example, electrical flash over was caused by a person entering in a clearance zone while circuit was live. Principle cause was unsafe act of entering in the clearance zone. Supplementary causes were lapse of management in electrical safety. Following questions were asked:

- Why the person was allowed to enter the clearance zone?
- Why safety fencing was not provided?
- Why the person was not aware of the risk?
- Why he was not trained?
- Who gave work permit?
- Why work permit was given without making the circuit dead earthed?

In conclusion: The accident was caused by lapse in safety system.

Principle 4

Unsafe acts and unsafe conditions can be identified in advance and eliminated at the root.

For example, a bare live conductor can be replaced by insulated cable. Oil filled transformer can be replaced by dry resin cast transformer, oil circuit breaker, can be replaced by vacuum circuit breaker.

Principle 5

For achieving ultimate safety, each link in the safety chain must be healthful. A single weak link makes the whole safety chain weak.

Safety links

- Plant design
- Equipment design
- Storage
- Civil works
- Erection
- Testing/Commissions
- Operation
- Maintenance
- Safety management

This is the concept of safety chain and safety link in construction industry. "Each safety link should be strong to make the safety chain safe."

Principle 6

Safety management system and human resource development in safety are the tools of every organization for ensuring safety.

For ensuring safety the company must have safety management systems. The employees and contractor persons must be trained to follow the safety management systems.

Principle 7

Safety is a line function in the organization.

The line refers to the line of authority viz. Managers, Supervisors, Workers. Each is responsible for creating safe conditions and for safe acts.

CONSTRUCTION SAFETY MANAGEMENT CHECKLIST

This checklist identifies some of the hazards most commonly found on construction sites. The questions it asks are intended to help the construction safety management.

Safe Places of Work

- Can everyone reach their place of work safely, e.g. are roads, gangways, passage ways, passenger hoists, staircases, ladders, and scaffolds in good condition?
- Are there guard rails or equivalent protection to stop falls from open edges or scaffolds, mobile elevating platforms, buildings, gangways, excavations, etc.?
- Are holes and openings securely guard railed, provided with an equivalent standard of edge protection or provided with fixed, clearly marked covers to prevent falls?
- Are structures stable, adequately braced and not overloaded?
- Are all working areas and walk ways leveled and free from obstructions such as stored materials and waste?
- Is the site tidy and are materials stored safely?
- Are there proper arrangements for collection and disposal of waste materials?
- Is the work adequately lit? is sufficient additional lighting provided when work is carried on after dark or inside buildings?

Scaffolds

- Are scaffolds erected, altered and dismantled by competent persons?
- Is there safe access to the scaffold platform?
- Are all uprights provided with base plates (and where necessary, timber sole plates) or prevented in some other way from slipping or sinking?

- Are all uprights, ledgers, braces and struts in position?
- Is the scaffold secured to the building or structure is enough places to prevent collapse?
- Are there adequate guard rails and toe boards or an equivalent standard or protection at every edge from which a person could fall 2 m or more?
- Where a guard rail and toe boards or similar are used:
  - Are the toe boards at least 150 mm in height?
  - Is the upper guard rail positioned at a height of at least 910 mm above the work area?
  - Are additional precautions, e.g., intermediate guard rails or brick guards in place to ensure that there is no unprotected gap of more than 470 mm between the toe board and upper guard rail?
- Are the working platforms fully boarded and are the boards arranged to avoid tipping or tripping?
- Are there effective barriers or warning notices in place to stop people using an incomplete scaffold, e.g., where working platforms are not fully boarded?
- Has the scaffold been designed and constructed to cope with the materials stored on it and are these distributed evenly?
- Does a competent person inspect the scaffold regularly, e.g., at least once a week; always it has been substantially altered, damaged and following extreme weather?
- Are the results of inspections recorded?

Powered Access Equipment

- Has the equipment been erected by a competent person?

- Is fixed equipment, e.g., mast climbers, rigidly connected to the structure against which it is operating?
- Does the working platform have adequate guard rails and toe boards or other barriers to prevent people and materials falling off?
- Have precautions been taken to prevent people being struck by the moving platform, projections from building or falling materials, e.g., barrier or fence around the base?
- Are the operators trained and competent?
- Are the power supply isolated and the equipment secured at the end of the working day?

Ladders

- Are ladders the right means of access for the job?
- Are all ladders in good condition?
- Are they secured to prevent them slipping side ways or outwards?
- Do ladders raise a sufficient height above their landing place? If not, are there hand holds available?
- Are the ladders positioned so that users do not have to over step or climb over obstacles to work?
- Does the ladder rest against a solid surface and not on fragile or insecure materials?

Roof Work

- Are there enough barriers and is there other edge protection to stop people or materials falling from roofs?
- Do the roof battens provide safe hand and tool holds? If not, are crawling ladders or boards provided and used?

- During industrial roofing, are precautions taken to stop people falling from the lending edge of the roof or from fragile or partially fixed sheets which could give way?
- Are suitable barriers guard rails or covers, etc. provided where people pass or work near fragile material such as asbestos cement sheets and roof lights?
- Are crawling boards provided where work on fragile materials can not be avoided?
- Are people excluded from the area below the roof work? If this is not possible, have additional precautions been taken to stop debris falling onto them?

Excavations

- Is an adequate supply of timber, trench sheets, props or other supporting material made available before excavation work begins?
- Is this material strong enough to support the sides?
- Is a safe method used for putting in the support, i.e., one that does not rely on people working within an unsupported trench?
- If the sides of the excavation are slopped back or battered, is the angle of batter sufficient to prevent collapse?
- Is there safe access to the excavation, e.g., by a sufficiently long, secured ladder?
- Are there guard rails or other equivalent protection to stop people falling in?
- Are properly secured stop blocks provided to prevent tipping vehicles falling in?
- Does the excavation affect the stability of neighboring structures?

- Are materials, spoil or plant stored away from the edge of the excavation in order to reduce the likelihood of a collapse of the side?
- Is the excavation inspected by a competent person at the start of every shift; and after any accidental collapse or event likely to have affected its stability?
- Has the risk of manual handling injuries been assessed?
- Are hoists, telehandlers, wheel-barrows and other plant or equipment used so that manual lifting and handling of heavy objects is kept to a minimum?
- Are materials such as cement ordered in 25 kg bags?
- Can the handling of heavy blocks be avoided?

Hoists

- Is the hoist protected by a substantial enclosure to prevent someone from being struck by any moving part of the hoist or falling down the hoist way?
- Are gates provided at all landings, including ground level?
- Are the gates kept shut except when the platform is at the landing?
- Are the controls arranged so that the hoist can be operated from one position only?
- Is the hoist operator trained and competent?
- Is the hoist's safe working load clearly marked?
- If the hoist is for materials only, is there a warning notice on the platform or cage to stop people riding on it?
- Is the hoist inspected weekly, and thoroughly examined every six months by a competent person?
- Are the results of inspection recorded?

Cranes and Lifting Appliances

- Is the crane on a firm level base?
- Are the safe working loads and corresponding radii known and considered before any lifting begins?
- If the crane has capacity of more than 1 tonne, does it have an automatic safe load indicator that is maintained and inspected weekly?
- Are all operators trained and competent?
- Has the banks man/slinger been trained to give signals and to attach loads correctly?
- Do the operator and banks man find out the weight and centre of gravity of the load before trying to lift it?
- Are cranes inspected weekly, and thoroughly examined every 14 months by a competent person?
- Are the results of inspections and examinations recorded?
- Does the crane have a current test certificate?

Plant and Machinery

- Is the right plant and machinery being used for the job?
- Are all dangerous parts guarded, e.g., exposed gears, chain drives, projecting engine shafts?
- Are guards secured and in good repair?
- Is the machinery maintained in good repair and are all safety devices operating correctly?
- Are all operators trained and competent?

Traffic and Vehicles

- Have separate pedestrian, vehicle access points and routs around the sites been provided? If not, are vehicle and pedestrians kept separate wherever possible?

- Have one way systems of turning points been provided to minimize the need for reversing?
- Where vehicles are to reverse, are they controlled by properly trained banks man?
- Are vehicles maintained; do the steering hand brake and foot brake work properly?
- Have drivers received proper training?
- Are vehicles securely loaded?
- Are passengers prevented from riding in dangerous positions?

FIRE AND EMERGENCIES

General

- Have emergency procedures been developed, e.g., evacuating the site in case of fire or rescue from a confined space?
- Are people on site aware of the procedures?
- Is there a means of raising the alarm and does it work?
- Are there adequate escape routes and are these kept clear?

Fire

- Is the quantity of flammable material on site kept to a minimum?
- Are there proper storage areas for flammable liquids and gases, e.g., LPG and Acetylene?
- Are containers and cylinders returned to the stores at the end of the shift?
- If liquids are transferred from their original containers? Are the new containers suitable for flammable materials?

- Is smoking banned in areas where gases or flammable liquids are stored and used? Are other ignition sources also prohibited?
- Are gas cylinders and associated equipment in good condition?
- When gas cylinders are not in use, are the valves fully closed?
- Are cylinders stored out side?
- Are adequate bins or skips provided for storing waste?
- Is flammable and combustible waste removed regularly?
- Are the right number and type of fire extinguishers available and accessible?

Hazardous Substances

- Have all harmful materials, e.g., asbestos, lead, solvents, paints etc. been identified?
- Have the risk to everyone who might be exposed to these substances been assessed?
- Have precautions been identified and put in place, e.g., is protective equipment provided and used; are workers and others who are not protected kept away from exposure?

Noise

- Are breakers and other plant or machinery fitted with silencers?
- Are barriers erected to reduce the spread of noise?
- Is work sequenced to minimize the number or people exposed to noise?
- Are others not involved in the work kept away?
- Is suitable hearing protection provided and worm in noisy areas?

Welfare

- Have suitable and sufficient numbers of toilets been provided and are they kept clean?
- Are there clean wash basins, warm water, soap and towels?
- Is suitable clothing provided for those who have to work in wet, dirty or otherwise adverse conditions?
- Are there facilities for changing, drying and storing clothes?
- Is drinking water provided?
- Is there a site hut or other accommodation where a worker can sit, make tea or prepare food?
- Is there adequate first-aid provision?
- Are welfare facilities easily and safely accessible to all who need to use them?

Protective Clothing

- Has adequate personal protective equipment, e.g., hard hats, safety boots, gloves, goggles, and dust masks been provided?
- Is the equipment in good condition and worn by all who need it?

Electricity

- Is the supply voltage for the tools and equipment the lowest, necessary for the job (could battery operated tools and reduced voltage systems, e.g., 110 V, or even lower in wet condition, be used)?
- Where mains voltage has to be used, are trip devices, e.g., residual current devices (RCDs) provided for all equipment?
- Are RCDs protected from damage, dust and dampness and checked daily by users?

- Are cables and leads protected from damage by sheathing, protective enclosures or by positioning away from causes of damage?
- Are the connections to the system properly made and are suitable plugs used?
- Is there an appropriate system of user checks, formal visual examinations by site managers and combined inspection and test by competent persons for all tools and equipment?
- Are scaffolders, roofers etc. or cranes or other plant, working near or under overhead lines? Has the electricity supply been turned off, or have other precautions, such as 'goal posts' or taped markers been provided to prevent them contacting the lines?
- Have underground electricity cables been located (with a cable locator and cable plans), marked and precautions for safe digging been taken?

Protecting the Public

- Are the public fenced off or otherwise protected from the work?
- When work has stopped for the day:
  - Are the gates secured?
  - Is the perimeter fencing secured and undamaged?
  - Are all ladders removed or their rungs boarded so that they can not be used?
  - Are excavations and openings securely covered or fenced off?
  - Is all plant immobilized to prevent unauthorized use?
  - Are bricks and materials safely stacked?
  - Are flammable or dangerous substances locked away in secure storage places?

Guidelines on Occupational Health and Safety Management for the Construction Industry

Some guidelines developed by Japan Construction Safety and Health Association (JCSHA) address the type of health and safety management system required of the construction safety industry, recognizing its special characteristics. Employees of construction industries may voluntarily adopt these management systems to promote safety and health at their construction sites.

Purpose

The purpose of these guidelines is to raise the level of safety and health in construction workplaces. To achieve this objective, these guidelines have been designed to encourage employers (contractors) to adopt, in co-operation with their employees, the four step process "Plan-Do-Check-Act" to reduce potential risks, promote employee's health and facilitate the establishment of a comfortable work environment.

Scope

These guidelines are applicable to all construction workplaces, regardless of size.

Terms and Definitions

The following terms that appear in these guide lines are defined therein:

Occupational Health and Safety Management Systems for Construction Industry (OHSMSCI), Construction Workplace, Contractor, Business Office, Project Site Office, Health and Safety Policy, Health and Safety Plan, Emergency Situation and Safety Audit.

General Requirements in Establishing 'OHSMSCI'

The guidelines catalogue the following general requirements at two levels, i.e., at business office and at project office, to be carried out by the contractors and project managers respectively in order to establish, implement and operate OHSMSCI.

- Declaration of health and safety policy.
- Identification of risks, hazards and countermeasures.
- Adoption of health and safety targets.
- Formulation of health and safety plan.
- Feedback employee's opinions in health and safety measures.
- Implementation and operation etc. of health and safety plans.
- Establishment of general procedures required at project site office.
- Establishing an organization for OHSMSCI.
- System education and training.
- Evaluation of Subcontractors' health and safety management capacities.
- Documentation.
- Emergency situations.
- Investigating causes of industrial accidents and determining the problems and formulating countermeasures.
- System audits.
- Records and their managements.
- Revisions to OHSMSCI.

Conclusion

The success of a construction safety management program depends on its people – how they are motivated and how they communicate with each other. One of the major key to success lies in establishing communication with people at all levels. Methods may include written circulars, reports, news sheets, safety promotional activities, incentive and or reward schemes, personal control and most success of all, structured safety meetings at the construction place where every one can become involved. Safety meetings at the construction place can be more fruitful, if a member of a group under the guidance of the management is asked to lead the meeting, having first been given the frame work of the subject for discussion and what the discussion hopes to achieve. All contractors of the work group should be included. Conclusions and concerns should be written down and acted upon as quickly as possible. The active participation of all contractors in safety meetings should be regarded as a long term objective. The main objectives of safety meetings are to:

- Seek ways to eliminate unsafe practices.
- Convey safety information to all the construction employees.
- Get participation in and commitment to the safety program.
- Encourage communication and debate.
- Resolve any concerns or problems that emerge.

Feedback should be given as soon as possible so that open action items do not accumulate. In addition to structured safety meetings, supervisors, when considering forthcoming jobs with their subordinates, need to discuss all the relevant safety aspects by means of a toolbox talk or pre job meeting.

A major management objective at both safety committee and safety meetings should be to find out how people at levels perceive the safety effort and whether safety information and messages are understood in the way they are meant. Feedback must be encouraged if people in the construction are to remain safe.

If management wants to reduce incidents and their related costs, everyone must place as much emphasis on safety as they place on other core activities. To be more effective safety must be balanced with all other core business activities. There must be a safety culture.

"Safety is number 1", or "Safety First" may sound good, but in reality, safety can not be considered separately from other aspects of the business. Rather it must become a basic value and not a priority for the management. Construction safety must consider changing "Safety is number one" and "Safety First" to "Safe construction with every body's attention" or something similar. The point is that a safety culture must be created and which should be valued by all construction employees.

Some core construction safety management points are:

- Safety and health are integral part of project construction.
- Teamwork is essential in all parts of construction.
- Managers and supervisors are out on the floor frequently and observe the construction safety rules.
- Employees are encouraged to identify safety related hazards and correct them on their own.
- Employees have full and open access to all the tools and equipment they need to do their job safely.

❐ ❐ ❐

CHAPTER 7

Construction Safety and The Statutory Provision

INTRODUCTION

Construction work is the core of development and progress whether it is the construction of new factories, dams, bridges etc. or major construction work connected with the expansion of a plant. Thus it is clear that construction plays an important role in the economical development of the country and that no progress is possible unless the construction proceeds according to the desired schedule. Impediments in the way of construction work are many, the accidents being a major one. The constructional activities throughout the country have been ever increasing. For the successful completion of construction work it is essential that proper attention be paid to the safety aspect.

There is no such thing as fate as far as accidents are concerned. The idea that accidents are unavoidable will always happen is wrong. In fact any accident can be avoided if the job is done in safe way and every one follows the safety rules.

Difference in the Safety in Operation and Construction Work

There is quite a difference between the safety during the operation and during the construction work. In the operating plant we have:

- Set procedures.
- The nature of work is repetitive.
- There is homogeneity of group working at a particular group.
- The hazards of the job and the necessary safety precautions to be taken are well known.

As against the above in a construction work we have:

- No set procedures of work.
- Changing pattern of day to day work.
- Different group of persons who have never worked together before.
- All the hazards of various jobs are not known to all the persons.
- A large number of persons of different trades work on different jobs simultaneously and at different levels of height.
- Rush of work and haste to complete the job ahead of the schedule with the result that sometimes shortcut methods are employed to save the time.
- A large number of skilled men of different trades are required with necessary physical standards. These are

sometimes difficult to meet with, with the result that persons with insufficient skills or previous experience in construction work are employed.

Thus we see that the hazards in the construction work are much more than in an operation work. It is therefore, all the more necessary that proper attention to safety should be paid during the planning of the construction work and the safety measures should be incorporated right from the start of the construction work.

Though there is a greater hazard in the construction work it has been shown by our experience that with proper planning and taking all the safety measures required, the construction work can be made as safe as an operation work.

Causes of Accidents in a Major Construction Work

Though the basic causes for the accidents are the unsafe acts on the part of the persons and the unsafe conditions, there are certain hazards which are peculiar to construction works which are listed below:

1. Materials falling from height.
2. Handling of heavy materials manually as well as mechanical.
3. Persons tripping and falling.
4. Persons falling from height.
5. Persons falling due to open pits or excavations on the ground.
6. Failure of lifting tools and tackles.
7. Collapse of scaffold, platforms.
8. Collapse of materials stacked.
9. Lack of proper communication and warning system between the work places at different levels.
10. Vehicular and rolling stocks accidents.

11. Shocks and burns from electricity.
12. Gas hazards (not applicable to all construction work).
13. Fire hazards.

As far as the unsafe acts on the part of the persons are concerned, these are mainly due to:

1. Lack of knowledge.
2. Tendency to save time and effort.
3. Personal worries such as the lack of housing facilities in construction work and the uncertainty for future jobs after a particular construction work is over.
4. Manual or physical deficiency.

The question naturally then arises that if the hazards of a construction job are so many, what can be done to ensure the safety of the personnel engaged on these jobs. Some of the points on which specific action could be taken before the construction work starts, are as follows:

1. Proper man power planning sufficiently in advance so that right type of persons with adequate knowledge and skill on the job can be selected.
2. Proper medical examination of all these persons for vision, blood pressure etc.
3. The induction of all persons to be engaged on the construction work. Special emphasis should be laid on this and all the hazards associated with that particular job should be properly explained to these persons and the various safety rules which must be observed should also be explained. Preferably a small booklet pointing the above should also be given to each and every worker after the same has been explained.
4. Incorporation of the safety measures during the planning of the construction work with regard to approaches to the work area and different places of

work , illumination, stacking of materials, disposal of waste and rejected material, prevention of fire, safety appliances necessary, permit to work certificate for work concerning gas, electricity and steam, warning signs and caution boards etc.

5. Safety training of the supervisors engaged on the construction work to look for the accident hazards, rectify them immediately to get the men to do the work in the safe way and to enforce the use of necessary safety appliances.
6. First-aid and rescue training and training in the use of fire extinguishers where necessary.
7. Supply of necessary safety appliances such as bolts, helmets, hand gloves etc. and to enforce their use.
8. Regular safety inspection of sites and elimination of any hazards noticed.
9. Discussion on safety matters in the daily progress meetings.
10. Prompt investigation of accidents if they take place and necessary action to be taken to prevent recurrence.

The safety officers attached to the construction work or in a department where a major construction work is going on, can help a great deal, in promoting safety on such jobs. The safety officers can be of particular help in the following aspects:

1. Proper induction of the men.
2. Inspection of the construction site to check any hazard enumerated above and any unsafe practice, so that these can be checked in time before they lead to an accident.
3. Holding meetings with workers, discussing safety matters and inviting suggestions from them.

4. Use of safety appliances.
5. Examination of lifting tackles.
6. Clearance certificates.

Check these in the Planning Stage

1. Construction site.
2. Transportation facilities such as rail road and plant road-ways.
3. Approaches and exits.
4. Walkways: floors, stairs, ramps, platforms etc.
5. Storage facilities for flammable and explosive materials, harmful substances, raw materials, finished products, and yard storage.
6. Electric wiring and installation.
7. Illumination.
8. Materials handling equipment such as cranes, conveyors, trucks and trolleys.
9. Elevators and lifts.
10. Boilers and other pressure equipment such as compressor.
11. Ventilation and dust control.
12. Fire control.
13. Health and safety related matters such as water for drinking and sanitary uses, waste disposal, medical and first aid service, and personal protective equipments.
14. Personal service facilities such as parking of vehicles etc., rest rooms, food service, employment and training.

CONSTRUCTION SAFETY ACT

Since construction industry is one of the oldest and most hazardous industries contributing to a high rate of fatalities and severe accidents statutory protection has now been provided through **building and other construction workers (regulation of employment and conditions of services) act, 1996.**

Objective of the Act

The Act has been made to provide safety, Health and Welfare measures and give construction workers a social security.

Responsibility of the Employer

The law requires that the employer should provide:

(a) A safe practice for work.

(b) A safe system for work.

(c) Safe access to and from the place of work.

(d) Safe plant and equipment.

Duties and Responsibilities of Worker

(a) Report the defects in the lifting devices/ gears without unreasonable delay.

(b) No building worker, shall unless duly authorized, remove or interfere with any fencing, gear, ladder, life saving appliances, covering, lighting or other things whatsoever required by the Act. If any aforesaid things are removed, the persons engaged in the work shall restore such things at the end of the period, during which its removal was necessary.

(c) Every building worker shall use only means of access provided in accordance with the rules.

(d) It shall be the duty of building worker to keep the latrines, urinals, washing points, canteen and other facilities provided by the employer, for securing his welfare, in a clear and hygienic condition.

Accident Prevention (Management Aspect)

1. Prepare a safety manual for the Project.
2. Depute full time/part time safety coordinators depending upon the size of the project site and nature of hazards.
3. Screening of workmen.
4. Prepare a project safety plan and implement at job sites which covers:
   (a) *Overall scope of work:* Fabrication, erection, excavation, concreting, brickwork, finishing work, painting, blasting, ND tests etc.
   (b) *Obligation chart:* Responsibility of the line functionaries and reporting of the safety engineering function.
   (c) *Safety committee:* (all job sites)
   - Structure: chairman, secretary and members.
   - Role and responsibilities.
   - Project manager.
   - Safety committee members.
   - Safety coordinators.
   - Site engineers.
   - First line supervisors, engineers.
   - Subcontractors.

   (d) Job related specific PPE.
   (e) General site safety rules:
   - Use of PPE and safety devices relevant to site activities.
   - General house keeping, stacking of materials.
   - Road safety inside the project.
   - Access/egress and work station safety.

- Safe use of construction power.
- Work permit system:
  - Hot work permit.
  - Excavation clearance permits.
  - Industrial radiography permit.
  - Permit to work on overhead traction line.
  - Permit to work on plant machinery and other power driven equipment.
  - Electrical work permit (HT & LT).
  - Permit to open manhole covers/grills.
  - Permit to confined space entry.

(f) Use, maintenance and inspection of plant and machinery.

(g) Scaffolding norms.

(h) Use of safe materials handling and personal handling equipment.

(i) Fire prevention and protection.

(j) Contingency plan.

(k) Others.

5. Identification of high risk/hazardous operations in the site and appropriate safety measures:

(a) Structural and equipment erection.

(b) Excavation.

(c) Concreting – chimney, silos, cooling towers etc.

(d) Pre-casting and pre-cast erection.

(e) Pile driving.

(f) Road work – existing roads/new roads.

(g) Work over water.

(h) Blasting.

(i) Use, handling, storage of compressed gas cylinders etc.

(j) Pressure testing – hydraulic and pneumatic.

(k) Tunneling.

(l) Others.

6. Pep talk.
7. Check lists and reports.
   - General site safety inspections: excavation, demolition, blasting, scaffoldings, ladders, working platforms, PPE, structural fabrication, and erection, gas cutting and welding, means of access, electrical work, house keeping, fire prevention and protection, road safety, first aid box, illumination, safety boards, posters, stickers, drinking water, sanitation, emergency vehicles.
   - Electrical safety inspection.
   - Erection safety inspection.
   - Scaffolding safety inspection.
   - Safety while working at height.
   - Cranes inspection.
   - Vehicle and earth moving equipment inspection.
8. Statistics and reports.
9. Accident investigation report:

   (a) Action taken report.

   (b) Weekly analysis of accidents.

   (c) Monthly safety statistics.

   (d) Register of first aid.

   (e) Sub-contractors' safety performance evaluation.
10. Job safety analysis:

Identity of Task: Asbestos roof sheeting at 25 meters height

Sl. No.	Sequence of operation activity steps	Hazards involved at various steps	Safety measures/ precautions	Responsibility/ action by
1.	Reaching to 25 meters height.	Slip and fall from height.	Approach ladders/stair case to be provided.	Execution Engineers.
2.	Walking on trusses and purlins.	Fall from height.	– Safety nets below. – Life line. – Mobile type fall arrestors. – Safety belts. – Crawling boards after providing the asbestos sheets. – Safety helmets. – Close super-vision.	Execution Engineers.

Date:

Signature: ---------------------- ---------------------------

Execution Engineer Safety Co-coordinators

11. Third Party (Competent Person) Inspection, Examination and testing of:
    (a) Hoists and lifts (Sec. 28), once in six months.
    (b) Lifting machines (crane, crab, winch, pulley blocks etc.) and lifting tackles (chain, rope, sling, hook, D-shackle, coupling, spider or similar appliances (Sec. 29), once in 12 months.

12. Safety training.
13. Safety awareness program.

BUILDING AND OTHER CONSTRUCTION WORKERS

(Regulation of Employment and Conditions of Service Central Rules 1998)

Definitions

Act: Means the Building and other construction workers' Act 1996/1998.

Safety: Safety may be defined as application of the Arts, Social & medical science, Education, Engineering and Law for prevention of accidents and conservation of health, life and property.

Project: A huge complex task involving capital investment, calibrated time, number of inter-related activities, unforeseen challenges and special safety arrangements is called project.

Construction: Construction in steel industry covers, civil works, structural, mechanical, electrical and refractory erection works including excavation, foundations, and the construction, structural alteration, renovation, modernization, major repairs, demolition, maintenance, fabrication, cleaning and painting etc.

Safe act: Safe act is planned event which is helpful to process, production and health of man, machine and material.

Base plate: Means a plate for distributing the load from a standard in the case of metal scaffolds.

Bay: In relation to scaffolds, means that portion of the scaffold between horizontal or vertical supports whether standards or supports from which the portion is suspended, which are adjacent longitudinally.

Brace: Means a member incorporated diagonally in a scaffold for stability.

Competent person: Means a person so approved by the Central Government, who belongs to a testing establishment in India, possessing adequate qualification, experience and skill for the purpose of testing, examination or annealing and certification of lifting appliances, lifting gears, wire ropes or pressure plant or equipment.

Compressed air: Means air mechanically raised to a pressure higher than atmospheric pressure at sea level.

Construction site: Means any site at which any of the processes or operation, related to building or other construction work, are carried on.

Conveyor: Means a mechanical device used in building or other construction work for transport of building material, articles, or packages or solid bulk from one point to another point.

Danger: Means danger of accident or of injury or to health.

Demolition work: Means the work incidental to or connected with the total or partial dismantling or razing of a building or a structure other than a building and includes the removing or dismantling of machines or other equipments.

Excavation: Means the removal of earth, rock or other material in connection with construction or demolition work.

False works: Means the structural supports and bracing for form works or forms.

Guard rail: Means a horizontal rail secured to uprights and erected along the exposed sides of scaffolds, floor openings, runways and gangways to prevent persons from falling.

Hazard: Means danger or potential danger.

Hazardous substance: Means any substance which due to its explosiveness, inflammability, radio-activity, toxic or corrosive properties, or other similar characteristics may

(i) cause injury, or

(ii) affect adversely the human system, or

(iii) cause loss of the life or damage to property or work-environment, while handling, transporting or storing and classified as such under the national standards or in case such national standards do not exist to the generally accepted international standards.

High pressure air: Means air used to supply power to pneumatic tools and devices.

Independent tied scaffold: Means a scaffold, the working platform of which is supported from the base by two or more rows of standards and which apart from the necessary ties stands completely free of the building.

Ledger: Means a member spanning horizontally and tying scaffolding longitudinally and which acts as a support for put logs or transform.

Lifting appliance: Means a crane, hoist derrick, winch, gin pole, sheer legs, jack, pulley block or other equipment used for lifting materials, objects or building worker.

Lifting gear: Means ropes, chains, hooks, slings and other accessories of a "Lifting appliance."

Magazine: Means a place in which explosives are stored or kept, whether above or below ground.

Man lock: Means any lock, other than a medical lock, used for the compression or decompression of persons entering or leaving a working chamber.

Material hoist: Means a power or manually operated and suspended platform or bucket operating in guide rails and used for raising or lowering material exclusively and operated and controlled from a point outside the conveyance.

Outrigger: Means a structure projecting beyond the façade of a building with the inner end being anchored and includes a cantilever or other support.

Put log: Means a horizontal member on which the board, plank or decking of a working platform are laid.

Responsible person: Means a person appointed by the employer to be responsible for the performance of specific duty or duties and who has sufficient knowledge and experience and the requisite authority for the proper performance of such duty or duties.

Right angle coupler: Means a coupler, other than a swivel or put log coupler, used for connecting tubes at right angles.

Scaffold: Means any temporarily provided structure on or from which building workers perform work in connection with building or other construction work to which these rules apply, and any temporarily provided structure which enables building workers to obtain access to or which enables materials to be taken to any place at which such work is performed, and includes any working platform, gangways, run, ladder or step ladder (other than a ladder or step ladder which does not form part of such structure) together with any guard-rail, tow board or other safe guards and all fixings, but does not include lifting appliance or a lifting machine or a structure used merely to support such an appliance or such a machine or to support other plant or equipment.

Sole plate: Means a member used to distribute the load from the base plate or the standard of wooden scaffolds to the supporting surface.

Sound or good construction: Means construction conforming to the relevant national standards or in case such national standard do not exist, to other generally accepted international engineering standards or code of practices.

Sound or good material: Means materials of a quality conforming to the relevant national standards or in case such national standards do not exist, to other generally accepted international engineering standards or code of practices.

Standard: Means a member used as a vertical support or column in the construction of scaffolds which transmits a load to the ground or to the solid construction.

Standard safe operating practices: Means the practices followed in building and other construction activities for the safety and health of workers and safe operation of machineries and equipment used in such activities and such practices conforms to all or any of the following, namely:

(i) Relevant standards approved by Bureau of Indian Standards.

(ii) National building code.

(iii) Manufacturer's instruction of safe use of equipment and machinery.

(iv) Code of practice on safety and health in construction industry published by International Labor Organization and amended from time to time

Suspended scaffold: Means a scaffold suspended by means of ropes or chains and capable of being raised or lowered but does not include a boatswain's chair or similar appliances.

Tie: Means an assembly used to connect a scaffold to a rigid anchorage.

Toe Board: Means a member fastened above a working platform, access landing, access way, wheel barrow run, ramp or other platform to prevent building workers and materials falling there from.

Transform: Means a member placed horizontally and used to transversely one ledger to another, or one standard to another in an independent tie scaffold.

Trestle scaffold: Includes a scaffold in which the supports for the platform are any of the following which are self-supporting, namely:

(i) Split heads

(ii) Folding

(iii) Step-ladder

(iv) Tripod

(v) Movable contrivances similar to any of the forgoing.

Tubular scaffold: Means a scaffold constructed from tubes and couplers.

Tunnel: Means a subterranean passage made by excavating beneath the over burden into which a building worker enters or is required to enter to work.

Working platform: Means a platform which is used to support building workers or materials and includes a working stage.

Workplace: Means all places where building workers are required to be present or to go for work and which are under the control of an employer.

❒ ❒ ❒

CHAPTER 8

Safety in Construction Industry

INTRODUCTION

Construction work is a high hazard occupation. Hence it is no surprise that construction workers are more prone to serious injuries and in some cases, fatalities, than other industries. That's why it needs the active safety measures. Because the accident frequency and severity rates in construction work are well above the average of all industries. In construction work safety aspects need proper consideration prior to construction, during the construction and after construction.

The responsibility shared by the owner and contractor in creating a construction with all safety standards for the protection of workforce and property from injury and damage. The idea is to minimize the hazards to the workforce and property of the owner and the contractor. The employer is responsible for providing a safe workplace for his employees. Simultaneously the employee is also responsible to follow whatever procedures are set up by his employer for his safety.

Prevention of accidents on construction site is mainly the responsibility of each concerned worker in respective areas of work. Knowingly or unknowingly performed unsafe acts of the concerned worker are 90% responsible for a major accident. The philosophy of safety should reach the grass root level so that safe working procedure becomes an integral part of our work culture.

SAFETY AT CONSTRUCTION SITE

In planning a construction the three most considerations are economy, speed and quality. Then the safety comes to the picture. This is the original concept of the construction through design. Good planning and hazard identification is essential to every element in execution of any construction. The challenge is to understand the hazards and to be sufficiently vigilant to take preventive action before an accident occurs.

ESSENTIALS OF ALL CONSTRUCTIONS

1. Appoint the right people.
2. Allow adequate time.
3. Provide information to the team.
4. Ensure proper communication and co-ordination.
5. Ensure suitable management arrangements are in its place.
6. Ensure adequate welfare facilities on site.
7. Ensure workplaces are designed correctly.
8. Appoint competent coordinators.
9. Appoint a principal contractor.

10. Ensure a health and safety plan in its place.
11. Keep the health and safety file.

HAZARDS AT CONSTRUCTION SITE

The work at construction site includes a large variety of activities, some of which are very hazardous. A good understanding of the hazards in various activities is essential for the worker who performs the work for the sake of total safety. Major construction hazards are given below.

Type of site activity/job	Hazard/risk involved	Remedy
1. Working at height	Giddiness, vertigo, falling down resulting in injury to self, slipping of tools, sparks and other materials resulting in injury to others, fall from openings etc.	Training, height pass, safety belt, platform with toe board, railing covering, and cordoning bottom area, trap trays.
2. Working in environment (a) inflammable gases (b) toxic gases	(a) Shock, fire/explosion resulting in injury/ loss of human life. (b) Intoxication, loss of consciousness, asphyxia, skin disorders, burning sensations.	Gas safety precautions -do-
3. Working with pneumatic tools	Loss of hearing due to noise pollution, various types of body injuries due to impact, dehydration due to sweating.	Use of ear plugs, training and plenty of fluid intake.
4. Metal work (a) Welding	Injury to eyes due to welding flash and/or scattering of slag, skin disorders, breathing	Welding screen, welding guards, hand gloves, nose cover, quality

Cont...

	problems due to welding fumes, burns due to hot materials, electric shock, fire hazards, etc.	holder, cleaning, and barricade below.
(b) Gas cutting	Injury to eyes, burns due to heat, skin disorders, fire hazards, breathing trouble, and back fire.	Use of goggles, hand gloves, barricading, back fire arrester.
(c) Machine work, e.g., grinding, drilling, cutting etc.	Body injuries due to scattering of sparks/ chips, electrocution due to improper electrical connections. Trapping.	Goggles, ear thing, light working dress, training.
5. Working in hot atmosphere	Burns, dehydration, exhaustion, risk of fire.	Training, blowers, extinguishers, fluid intake.
6. Installation/erection work	Body injuries due to improper use of handling equipment, ladders, scaffolding and/or use of defective tools, snapping slings, burning of wire rope or manila rope.	Training, testing and checking, never stand below load, safe approaches, trap trays, never overload.
7. Painting and other surface treatment	Skin disorders due to contact with paint and/or other chemicals, body injury due to accidental fall, eye injury due to falling of drops of paints and/or other foreign materials, lead poisoning.	Painting dress, Training, Safety height pass, Lot of milk intake.
8. Civil work (a) Excavation	Earth collapse, accidental fall, encounter with reptiles, electrocution due to U/G cables, fall of material from height, flooding of area.	Principle of shoring and railing, Training, Permission, Two approaches.

Cont...

(b) Blasting	Hazard of handling the explosives, body injuries due to splinters/sound/ earth collapse.	Training, Following the norms cf blasting.
(c) Site cleaning	Snake bites, Body injuries.	Training, Warning.
(d) Road work	Skin disorders, burns due to handling of hot bitumen, body injuries due to improper use of construction equipment and/or loose clothes.	Proper dress, Hand gloves, Gumboots, Training.
(e) Working under water	Drowning, shock, unconsciousness, suffocation.	Training, F rst-aid.
(f) Working in sewer lines.	Unconsciousness due to presence of poisonous gas, explosion.	Open manholes one hour before, training, safety belt, test for gases, never go alone.
(g) Roof/side sheeting work	Body injury due to accidental fall, shock, shock unconsciousness.	Height passes, training, Safety belts, Cat adders.
9. Working in dusty atmosphere	Throat and lungs congestion and breathing problems, injury due tc fall of foreign particles, suffocation.	Respirators, Nose covers, Blowers (fan).
10. Working in confined areas	Suffocation, Injury, Fire.	Training as per areas, Escape routs, Ventilation.
11. Working in electrical installations	Electrocution leading to death burns due to flash, shock/convulsion, accidental fall due to electric shock resulting in body injury.	Electric hand gloves, Mattress, First-aid training, Insulated tools, Work permit system.

SAFETY MEASURES DURING CONSTRUCTION

Safety management in general:

- Specific responsibility by name to be allotted at a specific point of time.

Planning of house keeping:

- The construction site must always be kept in neat and tidy condition. All materials must be stacked in proper place and in proper manner with proper marking.

A well planned site helps reduce accidents.

Safety while excavating:

- Provide side supports in an excavated trench.
- Always wear a safety helmet when you work in an excavation.
- Hand dig with care, as cables may be just below the surface.

Scaffolding:

- Make sure that scaffolds are securely anchored or tied to the building.

Ladders:

- Make sure your ladder is lashed or footed before you climb it.
- Avoid carrying tools or materials in your hand while you are climbing ladders.

Timber used in scaffolding and ladders should not be painted.

Movement of materials:

- While lifting the load through crane use a signaler and see that load is fitted with a safety hook.
- Never climb up the tower or get into the boom while the crane is in use.

- Never ride on the platform of a goods hoist.
- No one should stand within the operating area of the crane while the load is in motion.

Working positions, tools and equipments:

- Arrange to sit whenever possible.
- Keep materials, tools and controls within easy reach.
- Carry tools in tool holders and not in the pockets of clothing.
- A dangerous part of machinery requires guard – a warning notice is not a substitute.

Working environment:

- Never use solvents to remove paint or grease from your skin.
- The dust you cannot see is more dangerous than the dust you can see.

Personal protective equipment (PPE):

- Your safety helmet protects you only if you have it on.
- Ninety percent of all eye injuries can be prevented by suitable eye protection.
- Make a habit of using Personal Protective Equipment.

PREVENTING CONSTRUCTION ACCIDENTS

Major construction accidents at site were prevented by taking proactive actions such as heavy equipment accidents were prevented by:

- Developing operating procedures and their implementation.
- Employing trained and skilled persons to operate.
- Providing adequate signaling and supervision.
- Providing overload preventing devices.

- Installing warning devices such as back sensors, contact sensors, flashers equipped with warning buzzers.
- Periodic preventive maintenance and upkeep.

Landslide accidents, collapse of natural ground were prevented by maintaining a safe excavation grade and height and by constructing protective shoring.

Falling accidents were prevented by making work floors and pathways as flat and slip proof as possible and building handrails, fences in the work area, obstructing openings with scaffolding safety nets, safety ropes etc.

Providing nets, sheeting, reinforcement using bracing cable or other means prevented collapses of scaffolding/ structures.

Accidents caused by falling objects during construction work were prevented by construction plan that avoids work being performed in both high and low work areas at the same time, by using netting, construction sheeting, mesh sheeting, by binding materials together when placing them in high work areas, by building a drop chute and prohibiting access to hazardous area.

All workers were given appropriate personal protective equipments (PPE) while performing their jobs in order to protect their body parts from variety of hazards. Strict enforcement to use PPE (by both men and women) and maintenance of PPE resulted in significant reduction in minor injuries as well as reduction in number of first aid services.

Approach to be Adopted by Construction Industries

Safety cycle – The most powerful technique

1. **Morning safety ritual (daily everyone participating):** Every morning prior to work, all workers at site gather together and after physical exercises, a few

words are spoken by the site manager conveying the results of the previous day's inspection at the end of the day together with the orders of the day, pointers concerning safety measures for the day together with detailed directions deemed necessary for the day.

2. **Safety meeting:** Every morning before commencing work and right after the morning ritual, everyone is discussed to convene in-groups according to skills (scaffolding workers, carpenters for concrete molds, electrician's etc.) and the site manager indicates the tasks for the day, the special precautions concerning safety etc., are given orally to the respective workers concerned. Following which everyone speaks about foreseeable danger zones and precautions considered necessary for the day's work.

3. **Inspection prior to start of work:** Prior to starting work, the tools and machinery to be used for the day are inspected together with an inspection of the site.

   (i) **Inspection rounds of the site manager:** The Site Manager shall conduct inspection rounds checking conditions and in his spot-checking, shall give appropriate directions concerning safety precautions.

   (ii) **Directing and overseeing work in progress:** While work is progressing, the persons responsible for safety and health, the site manager and the site monitor shall direct and oversee the work of the staff and eliminate unsafe working conditions and also unsafe action taken by workers, etc.

   (iii) **Discuss safety procedures:** The main contractors and subcontractors (specialized skills) shall convene to discuss scheduling the following day's work (methods to be employed), the order of work together with safety measures to be employed.

(iv) **Cleaning up each area of responsibility:** All of the workers involved shall together before closing, clean up and put the whole site in order.

(v) **Checking site at close of work:** At the end of work, the safety monitor of the main contractor and the site managers of the specialist groups, etc. shall conduct checks on site for steps taken concerning prevention of fire, theft, third party injury, damage or accidents.

TYPES OF CHECK INVOLVED

Checklist System

1. **Electrical DB (Panel Board):** There is no safe voltage. All electrical equipment should consider dangerous. In a well laid system of electrical distribution, all the inbuilt safety provisions should be made. These include circuit breakers, double ear thing lightening arrester, tripping devices, etc. this should be maintained on monthly basis.
2. **Gas cylinder:** Contractor shall ensure gas cylinder safety at site during handling, transportation and storage. Use of flash back arrester on each set is must. Cylinder storage area is to be the 'no smoking' zone. Cylinders should be transported on trolleys in side the construction area.
3. **Welding machine:** All the welding machines are equipped with proper ELCB and ear thing. Welding machines are rested under the roof area. The bracings should not be used as ear thing. Each machine should have local ear thing.
4. **Chains, slings and ropes:** All the lifting accessories shall be tested periodically by the competent person.

The fitness certificates are to be submitted to owner/principal contractor. Periodical checking of these items are to be done by the contractor.

5. **Scaffolding:** It is an essential requirement of any construction work. It should have proper approaches, working platform, proper hand railing, toe boards, etc. Its loading should be vertically above the standards or at specially structured loading bays. This is to be maintained on fortnightly basis.
6. **Structural erection:** For this purpose properly trained, experienced and equipped workers are allowed. Sufficient fall arresting systems, full body harnesses are to be provided. Area to be properly barricaded.
7. **Excavation:** It has a potential for injury. Area should be properly fenced, danger sign posted and properly illuminated at night. The sides of excavated area should be properly slopped or bench cut and adequately shored. The cutting soil should be dumped at least 1.5 meters from the edge of trench. This is to be maintained on weekly basis.
8. **Cranes and hydra:** All cranes and hydras should be load tested by the competent person. All are having safe load indicator, load chart, boom angle indicator, limit switch, etc. The operator should be sufficiently experienced.
9. **House keeping:** It is not just push broom method. It is a practical method of reducing accidents, increasing production and improving employee moral. It is necessary to provide proper lay out of work area for storage of materials and collection point of debris.
10. **Winch and hoisting system:** All winch and hoisting systems should be load tested by the competent per-

son. All are having safe working load, brake, limit switch, emergency push button, connected with 30 mA ELCB/RCCB, etc. The operator should be sufficiently experienced.

Training

1. **Induction/Orientation:** Contractor will ensure induction training to all his personnel after taking entrance in to the project site. The training should be imparted in a language understood by them. They should be trained about the potential hazards and their measures. The topic should cover all the safety aspects related to the project area.
2. **Tool box/Pep talk:** It is to be conducted by the immediate supervisor to the gang/crew before starting day's activity on the daily basis. In this programme he will explain the related hazards with the job and their safety measures. Also any forthcoming safety hazards, events, instructions, orders, etc. given to the crew during this program. This program should be done in local language.
3. **Awareness/refresher:** Periodically educating and training the supervisors and workmen in general safety, fire fighting, first aid, emergency system, house keeping, etc. It will go a long way in preventing many common accidents at construction site.
4. **On the job:** This type of training are organized by the contractor/principal contractor/client to train a particular group of workers on their running job. It helps the workmen to know practically about the safe/unsafe practices involved with their job.
5. **Specialized or class room:** The client/principal contractor should arrange this type of training programs on specific topic like, height work, fire fighting, electrical welding, gas cutting, etc.

6. **Live demonstration:** The client/principal contractor should arrange live demonstrations on fire fighting system, use of fall arresting and safety harness system, use of fire extinguisher, first-aid, etc.

Health Check Up

1. **During getting the gate pass:** In other word this health check up is meant for screening. It is very much essential to identify physical handicaps like deafness, defective vision, BP, epilepsy, etc. It is a must to place the right person on right job.
2. **During screening for Height job:** A special organized health check up program organized by the client to find out the physically fit workers for the height work. These sort-out workers are only allowed for the height work and issued a height pass.

Work Permit System

1. **Excavation work:** Prior to start the excavation, it must be planned and checked properly. So that the arrangements are made to locate underground services, establish ground conditions and design adequate support systems. Also check whether the excavation will destabilize any existing structure.
2. **Cold work:** Any activity other than hot work like material handling, transportation, vehicle movement, etc. needs cold work permit.
3. **Working at height/elevation:** For the work above 3 meters height the contractor shall issue a height permit. It should be properly verified and certified by the concerned authority. The contractor shall be given undertaking to ensure all the safety measures during the work.

4. **Night work:** Only in some special cases this permit can be issued. Contractor must ensure about the safe practices along with all statutory safety requirements. Contractor maintains this permit date wise and keeps the record. This permit is valid for 15 days only.
5. **Confined space entry:** Entry into the confined space can be permitted only when all necessary tests have been properly conducted or recorded. Rescue arrangements and necessary procedures have been planned properly and all concerned know them. Properly trained and suitably equipped persons must remain at the entrance of the confined space for the duration of work.
6. **Hot work:** All type of hot work come under this permit. Contractor must provide all related fire fighting arrangements. All the adequate safety appliances are to be provided. The workmen are well trained and experienced about this type of work. This permit is valid for 7 days only.
7. **Controlled blasting:** Only on exceptional cases this permit can be given subjected to the prior permission taken from the local authority in writing. Only the licensed blaster should carry out blasting activity. This permit is valid for a single case only.
8. **Erection work:** Any erection job involving hot and cold work which is carrying out at height or ground level or at any platform level. Contractor produces the approved erection plan and safe plan of action along with the permit asked for. The contractor shall be given undertaking to ensure all the safety measures during the work.

PERSONAL PROTECTIVE EQUIPMENT (PPE)

Contractor shall provide 100% PPE's to their staffs and workers, their sub-contractor's and ensure the use at site. The issue of PPEs should be registered and production of the same is required to the inspection team on demand. All the PPEs should cover the IS standard specification. It is mandatory that any one permitted to enter the work area, wear safety helmet and safety shoes.

All personnel on site must wear the basic personal protective equipment specific to their work. These are:

- For head protection – **Safety helmet**
- For foot protection – **Safety shoes**
- For eye protection – **Safety goggles**
- For hand protection – **Hand gloves**
- For body protection – **Apron**
- For fall protection – **Safety harness**
- For ear protection – **Ear plug/muff**
- For respiratory protection – **Nose mask**

Site Safety Inspection

To eliminate the potential hazards at site, periodical safety inspections shall be carried out regularly by:

1. Daily Inspection
2. Joint Inspection with client.

Safety Audit

It involves reviewing the entire safety plan/systems which are already in place and to review its effectiveness. Various safety audits can be undertaken at construction sites are:

1. Internal/external HSE audit
2. OHSAS audit

3. Departmental HSE audit
4. Divisional audit.

Incident/Accident Investigation

The purpose of investigation is to collect information and interpret related causes to discover the points of failure, so that the proper and adequate action can be taken to prevent a recurrence. This must be for fact finding, not for fault finding. An investigation procedure followed by:

1. Primary investigation
2. Secondary investigation
3. Reporting by committee
4. Implementation of recommendation

Safety Promotional Activity

1. Safety quiz competition
2. Safety poster competition
3. Safety slogan competition
4. Award for Best Agency/Contractor
5. Award for Best Worker(s)
6. Award for Best Engineer/Supervisor

Documents/Record Keeping

Contractor shall develop a fully planned documented system for implementation and monitoring the safety aspects:

1. Register of adult workers
2. PPEs issue Register
3. First-aid register
4. Monthly HSE related reports
5. Tool box talk/PEP talk register
6. Load test certificates

7. Training reports
8. Register of accidents and dangerous occurrences.

Conclusion

Prevention of accidents on construction sites is the responsibility of each concerned employee in respective areas of work. The philosophy of safety should reach the grass root level so that safe working procedure becomes an integral part of our work culture. The engineers, supervisors and workmen all need to know the task to be undertaken towards formulating a safety culture in construction industry.

So incorporating the safety in all construction phases in a structured and concerted manner is a must.

❐ ❐ ❐

CHAPTER 9

Safe Rigging Practice in Construction Industry

FUNDAMENTALS

The art and science of rigging may be traced back to prehistoric times when levers were used to pry heavy objects and inclined plane to help move heavy loads to higher levels. One of the examples of heavy rigging work is the gigantic pyramid at Giza near Cairo (Egypt) built about 2700 B.C. which is 764 ft. square at the base and 480 ft. high. About 2⅓ million stones from 2 to 30 tons in weight each were transported from the quarry to the Nile River at the flood season, ferried across the river on rafts, dragged from river to the site of the pyramid and piled up on each other to a height of a 40 storied building. The accomplishment of the Egyptians is almost unbelievable for the times when they had no cranes, chain hoists, jacks and other mechanical devices. It is believed by some historians that a ramp was built up one side of the pyramid and the stones were dragged up the slope by slaves working in teams.

A relatively simple job as lifting a piece of machinery to the second floor of a building may call for ropes, slings, hooks, timbers, chain blocks, rollers, pulley blocks, crow bars, scaffolding and so forth. Rigging also includes erecting temporary scaffolds for painting, repairs or demolishing structures as well as for supporting heavy loads. In the rigging trade there is no substitute for years of practical experience. But when working by rule of thumb alone, many times ropes and other load bearing parts are stressed to a point dangerously close to breaking point without the rigger realizing it. Therefore those in the rigging trade must be able to make simple calculations to check their loads and strength of their equipments.

The elementary machines from which mechanical advantage is obtained are the inclined plane, the lever, the gearing system and the block and fall.

Fiber Rope

Use had been made at various times of such materials as fibrous bark of palm tree, the coir of the coconut, camel hair, horse hair, thongs cut from hides, cotton, jute flax and wild and cultivated hump, until to-day we have the modern manila and sisal rope.

While wire rope may be considered an improvement over fiber rope, it has not entirely superseded fiber rope for each has its own field of use. Wire rope is generally used for lifting heavy loads and for permanent installations. Fiber rope, on the other hand, is used for light loads and for construction and painting jobs and for marine works. Wire rope has a known strength, but fiber rope can not have the exact calculated strength as fiber is a product of nature and its strength is dependent on climatic conditions, fertility of soil, cultivation land curing.

Tools and Tackles Used in Rigging

Rigging includes lifting and erecting heavy machineries & structural.

The different tools and tackles used in Rigging Work are:

1. Ropes
   - Fiber ropes
   - Wire ropes
2. Slings
3. Hooks
4. Timbers
5. Chain blocks
6. Rollers
7. Pulley blocks
8. Crow bars
9. Scaffoldings
10. Inclined plane
11. Levers
12. Gearing system
13. Winch
14. Jacks
15. Cranes
16. Derricks
17. Ladders
18. Chains
19. Hoists

Fiber Rope

Manila and Sisal ropes are in extensive use. These are fiber ropes. Wire rope is an improvement over fiber ropes. Due to some of the advantages of fiber ropes wire rope can not totally supersede the use of fiber rope.

Comparison

Wire Rope	Fiber Rope
1. Wire rope is generally used for lifting heavy loads and for permanent installations	1. Fiber rope is preferred for light loads and for painting jobs, also for marine works.
2. Wire rope has a known strength.	2. Fiber rope can not have the exact calculated strength as

	fiber is a product of nature and its strength is dependent on climatic conditions, fertility of soil, cultivation and curing.

Hints on Handling and Use of Fiber Rope

Here are some important points in the use of fiber rope:

1. Fiber rope should never be kept on the floor or in a box, closed or small room where air is restricted. It should be hung up in loose coils on large diameter wooden pegs. Rope should be protected from weather and from dampness. A wet rope should be thoroughly dried and cleaned before being stored away. It should be kept away from boilers, radiators, steam pipes and other sources of heat. Exposure to stack gases, acid fumes, carbon monoxide or carbon dioxide will cause rapid deterioration of the rope.
2. When a rope is attached to a hook, ring or pulley block, a thimble should be placed in the loop or eye to reduce the wear on the rope and to decrease the stresses developed in the rope when it is bent round a very small diameter.
3. When the rope is used as a sling, it should not pass over sharp edges of castings, beams etc., proper padding should be used. Also consideration should be given to the angles between the legs of a sling. (If ropes make an angle of 60 degree to the horizontal they have only 86% of their strength when vertical, 71% at 45 degree and 50% at 30 degree).
4. Rope should not be dragged on ground as it will be worn by abrasive action. Also small particles of gritty material may get between the component parts of the rope and cause damage.

5. Fiber ropes used between fixed objects such as in the case of guys on a gin pole should be slackened when it rains; otherwise shrinkage may overstrain the wet rope and damage it.
6. Fiber rope should be inspected thoroughly before and after use. Like the proverbial chain, a rope is only as strong as its weakest part and it is user's duty to find that part. The outside of the rope as well as the inside of it (by untwisting the strands) should be examined by going over each foot of the rope. A rope upon which a man expects to trust his life should not be inspected in any but the most thorough manner. Accumulation of powder like saw dust inside the rope indicates excessive internal wear. Excessive oil on the outside of a new rope is also an indication that it has been overloaded. If the inside of a rope is dirty, if the strands have begun to unlay, or if the rope has lost its 'life' and elasticity, it should not be used for hoisting proposes.
7. When a rope has been condemned, it should be destroyed at once or cut up into short hand lines so that it can not again be used for hoisting.
8. For opening a new coil of rope, the end of the rope should be at the bottom of the core or eye and the end should be pulled out through the core. If this is not followed kinks will be formed which will damage the rope.
9. When a rope is cut to the required length, whippings of yarn should be applied at once to the ends to prevent the strands from becoming unlayed.
10. If the rope is used for lifting loads with pulley blocks, it is advisable to reverse the ends periodically so that the rope is worn out more or less uniformly through out.

Knots, Bends and Hitches

A 'Knot' is the intertwining of the end of a rope with a portion of a rope. A 'Bend' is the intertwining of the ends of two ropes to make one continuous rope. A hitch is the attachment of a rope to a post, pole ring hook or other object. A 'splice' is the joining of the ends of two ropes or of the end of a rope with the body of the rope by wearing the strands over and under the strands of the other part.

Wire Rope

A wire rope is usually made up of a number of wires laid left or right handed into a strand and number of strands, usually 6 or 8, laid right or left handed round a hemp rope centre to form the wire rope, or steel cable as it is generally called. There are four different ways of laying the rope as given below.

Construction

There are a great number of different possible constructions of wire rope. These are described by indicating first the number of strands, then the number of wires in each strand, namely 6 × 7, 6 × 19 or 6 × 37. The smaller (and more numerous) the wires the more flexible the rope but the less resistant to external abrasion.

Preforming

A preformed rope is one in which the wire when laid into strands and strands when laid into rope are slightly bent beyond the elastic limit in the curve so that they spring back only slightly and when such a rope is cut the wires and strands do not unlay.

Grades of Steel

Wire ropes are manufactured in the following grades or strength ranges. In the order of decreasing strength these are as follows:

1. *Extra improved plow steel* – very high strength.
2. *Improved plow steel* – high strength, wear resistant, tough, best fatigue life.
3. *Plow steel* – for moderate service requirements.
4. *Traction steel* – for passenger and freight elevators.
5. *Iron wire rope* – Low tensile strength, soft and ductile; used for stationary guy lines etc.

Wire Rope Cores

Wire ropes are available with different cores around which the strands are laid and the core has the important function of supporting the strands in their relative positions throughout the life of the rope. Fiber core is most widely used. Fiber provides a resilient cushion for the several strands and does not cross nick the outer wires of the strand next to the core. When normal operating loads are so great that fibers rupture, a steel core becomes necessary. Wire cores are of two common types: (i) a small rope (independent wire rope core) and (ii) a multiple wire strand (wire strand core). Ropes with independent wire rope cores are practically equal in flexibility to those with fiber cores and may be selected in cases where relative small sheaves and drums are used. The wire strand core being smoother and more solid provides better support for rope strands and is required to be used where operating loads and bearing pressures are extremely high, but is not suitable for use on small sheaves and drums as it is less flexible.

Proper Use of Wire Rope

Here are some of the important points for proper use of wire rope:

1. Wire rope should be stored in a cool dry place away from local heat, fumes, chemicals, dampness etc.

2. It should be kept in a reel or spool until used. If it is to be stored for a long time, the outer layer should be coated with moisture resistant lubricant.
3. When a length of rope is removed from its spool, it is important that the spool be rotated either on a spindle resting on trunnions or small turn table. The rope should come out without kinks. Care should be taken so that slack will not get into the turns on the reel and bend round the shaft. If this happens and a kink is formed the rope is ruined at that point.
4. The correct way to unreel wire rope is one man must hold the end of the rope, while the second man rotates the reel allowing the rope to unreel naturally with the lay, without spiraling or twisting.
5. Once a kink is formed in a rope, no amount of twisting or strain can completely remove it and the rope is weakened and may be unsafe for use.
6. Before cutting any wire rope (including preformed rope), it is essential to apply seizing either side of the proposed cut. The rope should never be cut first and then seized. If cutting is done by means of oxy-acetylene torch, the wires and strands may be welded simultaneously.
7. The wire rope may be cut by oxy-acetylene torch, mechanical shear or with an abrasive cutting wheel. In a construction the first method is most common.
8. It is important that wire rope be attached at the correct locations of flat or smooth face drums in order to have it spooled evenly with the turns laying snugly against each other and with even layers. If the rope is started incorrectly, the turns in first layers may spread with resultant flattening or crushing of the rope when succeeding layers are spooled. A simple method of

deciding how a rope can be started on a drum is by use of right or left hand as is clearly enclosed in figure at the end of the chapter.

9. The right and the wrong ways of attaching U-bolt wire rope clips (or crossly clips) are enclosed in figure at the end of the chapter. In the right method, the base of the clip bears against the live of the rope while the 'U' of the bolt presses against the dead end. The clips are usually spaced about six rope diameters apart to give adequate holding power. A wire rope thimble should be used in the loop eye to prevent kinking. To attach clips, bind the rope on itself at toe of the thimble. Then apply the clip farthest from the thimble first at about 4 inch from the end of the rope, and screw up tightly. Next put on the clip nearest the thimble and apply the nuts hand tight. Then put one or more intermediate clips hand tight. Take a strain on the rope and while the rope is under this strain, tighten all the clips previously left loose. Take a turn alternately on the two nuts to keep the riddle of the clip square. No slackness should exist in either part of the rope between the clips. After the rope has been in operation for a short time it is a good practice to tighten up the clips again. The correct number of clips for safe application and spacing distances are given in figure at the end of the chapter.

10. To reduce to a safe figure the load on the cable anchorage on a drum, it is necessary to leave at least two and preferably three complete wraps of rope on the drum. If the load carried by the rope is 1000 lbs, the load on the cable anchorage with 3 wraps will be 220 lbs for a well greased rope and as low as 34 lbs for a dry rope.

11. There is a regular procedure for attaching wire rope sockets (with zinc) which should be followed and must be done by competent men.

Inspection

It is poor economy to discard an expensive rope before it is necessary. Likewise, it is dangerous (and it may even prove even more expensive) to continue its use beyond a certain stage. To determine the proper time to condemn the rope a careful inspection is necessary.

(i) **Broken wires:** The total number of wires in all the strands within a distance of one rope lay (i.e., the distance in which a strand makes one complete turn around a rope) at the portion of rope is taken as an index of reduction in strength due to this case.

(ii) **Wear on outside wires:** The length of the shiny worn spots on the outside wires is an indication of the reduction in area, and likewise in the strength of the wires and of the rope due to wear. Maximum wear allowed on outside wires is 33% for most cases.

(iii) **Weak points:** The weakest part of a rope, like the proverbial chain determines the strength of the rope. This weak point may be where the rope is badly worn, where it has a number of broken wires, where the local stresses due to bending the rope over a sheave are excessive or where the rope is attached to the equipment. This should be thoroughly inspected.

Slings, Hooks, Hoisting Chains, Shackles

Slings

Various materials can be used for slings. For very light loads an endless fiber rope looped into a noose around the object to be lifted is satisfactory. Such a sling is inexpensive, of light weight flexible and easy to handle. It can be bent round the comparatively sharp edges of boxes or crates but should be padded when passing over the sharp machined edges or metal parts. Even on some heavier jobs, such as handling of steel shafts which must not be scratched or burred fiber rope slings are advantageously used.

For special work, slings are sometimes made of other materials such as roller chains, leather and cotton webbing, but by far the most popular is the wire rope sling. The main advantage of a wire rope sling is that a core rope of say 6 × 19 construction consists of 6 strands, each containing 19 wires, laid around a hump core and if there is a failure of one component (a wire), there will be a reduction in strength of less than 1% which is insignificant where as it will be a total failure in a chain. But still, wire rope slings must be carefully chosen for the service in which they are to be placed, as they also have certain limitations. Hereunder are some points which should be borne in mind.

1. Like manila rope and chain slings, wire rope slings must be padded where being bent over sharp edges of the object to be lifted.
2. Wire rope slings must not be allowed to become kinked. This accounts for many sling failures.
3. Slings of 1/2 in. and above should be made from wire rope with an independent wire rope centre. This will reduce the possibility of the rope being crushed in service.
4. The very large sizes are often made of 6 × 37 or 6 × 6 × 19 construction to increase the flexibility.
5. All slings that have at one time or another been bent sharply become 'cranky ' (i.e., they develop permanent deflections) so that when strain is removed they will snarl.
6. Slings made of preformed rope behave some what better than those made in the conventional manner and also have the advantage that broken wires will not so readily wicker out and present a hand hazard

to the rigger, but tend to lay 'dead' on the original position.

There are a wide variety of slings, but endless slings and a single sling are most common. There are different ways of slinging of handling different materials. A sling can be used as a basket sling or single choker. Two of these slings can be used as a pair known as a two leg sling or a double basket sling or a double choke sling. Such slings should never be bent around small diameters or passed over sharp edges of the load.

All slings should be made of improved plow steel rope. All eye splices should be made by experienced splicers and should be properly served to conceal the sharp protruding ends of the wires which frequently cause injury to the riggers handling them. It is a good practice to place thimbles in all spliced eyes. When not in use, slings should be hung up in an orderly manner on special hooks or brackets so as to keep them as straight as possible. Special consideration should be given to those legs of the spring make to the horizontal. At 60 degree the lifting capacity is 87% of that of vertical, at 45 degree it is 71% and at 30% it is only 50%. Slings should be inspected periodically and condemned when found in unsafe condition. They should be protected from corrosion and from contact with injurious chemicals.With reasonable care a sling should last indefinitely and should be one of the safest parts of the hoisting equipment.

Hooks

Only standard hooks should be used for hoisting. The hook should be the weakest part of any crane, hoist or sling. It seldom breaks, but it may fail by straightening out and finally releasing the load. A distorted hook is prima-facie evidence of overloading. Reforging and/or annealing of spread hooks are not permitted. When inspecting a hook particular attention must be paid to the small radius fillets at the neck.

Chains

Chains made from high grade wrought-iron are widely used because of its extreme ductility, wrought iron has a large shock-absorbing capacity and chains made of this material will stretch considerably under an overload unless they have been over strength or the links embrittled. Wrought-iron has additional advantage that it is easily welded. Welded chains of nickel steel are also used where exacting requirements must be met.

According to the existing regulations all chains in use in construction have to be sent to shops for annealing and testing once in a period of 6 months and a proper record indicating the chain number, date put in service, date sent to shops for annealing and testing, date received back from shops is required to be maintained by the using departments. When ever any chain fails in service, investigations are carried out by the metallurgist and reason for failure is determined. Broken chains are repaired only at the shop to ensure a proper job.

The common type of defects that occur to chains in use are: (a) dents or cuts due to rubbing against hard and sharp surfaces (b) wear of links by friction (c) elongation due to over loading; or shock (d) progressive opening or decay of welds (e) pitting and corrosion of links (f) deformations due to twisting and (g) disturbance in normal structure due to contact with hot materials. Inspection of chains should be carried out at least once a month keeping the chains hanging vertically. Dents, pits and elongation in length can easily be detected. Reduction in cross section should be measured and a reduction of 20% or 1/16 in may be considered sufficient indication for rejecting the link. Inspection of all welds is necessary as more failures occur at welds than any where else.

The main cause of failure of chains is overloading which must be avoided. When two or more chain are used for lifting a load the angle to the horizontal at which the chains are used determines the load carried by the chain and it may be mentioned that at 30 degree angle the load is double. Also shock loads far in excess of the breaking loads can occur due to sudden stopping while lifting or lowering loads which should be avoided.

All chains can be safely used at temperatures between 48° F and 600° F as there is very little drop in strength up to the upper limit. Above this temperature there is a rapid decrease in strength. Chains also become shock sensitive below the freezing point.

Chains must be stocked under cover and should hang vertically from pegs in atmosphere free from dust, moisture and corrosive fumes.

Chain Hoists, Jacks and Pulley Blocks

Chain Blocks

These are portable lifting devices suspended from a hook and operated by hand chain. They are used for short lifts and for intermittent service on loads up to 10 tons usually.

Three types are in use each being provided with a hook to suspend the hoist from the overhead member, hook and chains for supporting the load and hand chain for imparting power.

The "differential hoist" consists of three chain sheaves with an endless chain for lifting and operating. One of the upper sheaves is constructed with an extra link pocket. The difference in diameter being too small to overbalance the friction of the parts, the load is automatically sustained at any point making the hoist self locking.

The "worm-geared hoist" consists of an operating chain passing over a pocket sheave mounted on worm shaft. The worm imparts motion to the two load sheaves; the load chain is attached to the swivel hook and passes over the load sheaves, the slack hanging in a loop. The worm-gear makes the hoist self locking. Separate chains are used for hoisting and operating.

The "Spur-gear hoist" has a higher efficiency than the other types and to sustain the load a mechanical brake, consisting of a ratchet pawl and friction plate is used. Two separate chains are used one for hoisting and one for operating. To lower, the hand chain is pulled in reverse direction.

Here are some hints for proper use of chain blocks:

1. Never drag the chain block on the floor; it should be carried.
2. Chain blocks when not in use should be hung on hooks and kept under cover and not left on floor.
3. Chain blocks must be inspected before and after use in the interest of safety.
4. Lubricate chain blocks periodically.
5. Once a year or oftener strip off the block completely. Examine all parts thoroughly and change worn out parts. Hook and chain should be checked with standard gauges. Proper records of such inspections are required to be maintained.
6. While drawing chain blocks from stores, insist on getting the test certificate for it and preserve it.
7. Number all chain blocks in the site. Keep proper service records of the same.
8. The load capacities should never be exceeded. It is advisable to lift 10% less load than specified. Jerks while lifting should be avoided.

Chain Blocks

These are roller chain hoists with a ratchet handle for operating and have 3 to 6 feet lifts. Such hoists are light and can be handled by one man and thus have a definite advantage over the chain block for short lifts and pulls in erection and maintenance work.

Jacks

Jacks are portable tools for lifting heavy loads through short distances. There are several types of jacks:

1. Screw jack
2. Screw jack with ratchet handle
3. Rack and lever jack
4. Journal jack
5. Hydraulic jack with built-in pump
6. Hydraulic jack with separate pump and flexible connection
7. Traversing jack
8. Foot lift or toe jacks

The jacks most commonly used are of types 4, 5, 6 and 7. For any use the following instructions should be followed:

(a) Choose jack of at least 25% higher capacity than the load to be lifted.

(b) Use wooden blocks below and above the jack to reduce chances of slipping, the head should bear squarely under the load to be lifted; if not, use taper wooden packings.

(c) Use same capacity and type of jacks when a load is to be lifted by 2 or more jacks and work up or down the jacks simultaneously.

(d) Inspect, clean and lubricate jacks before and after use.

(e) Handle jacks carefully to avoid any damage and never drag on floor.

(f) When not in use store jacks properly in racks after applying a thin layer of grease to prevent rusting.

(g) Use jacks according to instructions provided by the manufactures. All jacks have a mark on the ram indicating the limit of ram travel which should never be exceeded.

(h) Always use clean oil of given specifications on hydraulic jacks.

(i) Use standard length levers provided with hydraulic jack and not any available bar.

(j) There are some hydraulic jacks meant to be used in vertical position only which should not be used in horizontal position.

Pulley Blocks

Fiber rope pulley blocks 3/8 in to 1 in sizes. Single and double sheaves are stocked in the stores. Only pulley blocks conforming to Indian Standard specifications are purchased and each block is accompanied by a test certificate. Project sites using these blocks are required to maintain a register giving the serial number, size, safe working load, and date put in service, date of inspection, defects if any, by whom inspected. Accordingly to Factories Act, these blocks are required to be inspected at least once a year and before 15th December every year a report on the same is expected to be submitted to the Inspector of Factories.

The parts to be inspected are the hook, axle, pin, sheaves, bucket and the bucket pin. The block should be stripped off and parts examined carefully. If the hook has opened out, sheave flanges broken or axle pin worn out more than 10%, the block should be rejected outright.

The pulley blocks should be stocked under cover and hung on hooks.

Scaffolding, Ladders, Cranes, Hoists and Derricks

Scaffolding

Common types of scaffolding used are:

(a) Partially fabricated steel scaffolding in which welded tubular frames are stood up opposite each other and the removable cross braces installed between them are placed on stud bolts which are welded to and form an integral part of the frame. After the first tier of panels is erected, the second sets of frames are shocketed in to their upper ends.

(b) Tubular steel scaffolding which consists of steel tubing of about 2 in. O.D. in lengths of 6, 8, 10 and 13 ft. and used for poles ledgers, bearers and bracing. Special clamps or couplers are used to fasten tubes to one another.

(c) Temporary wood scaffolds of sizes 6 ft. × 4 ft., 4 ft. × 2 ft. and 3 ft. × 2 ft. In which the decking planks are nailed to wooden beams below and scaffold is suspended by 4 pieces of fiber rope. This is particularly suited for 1 to 2 persons working on steel structures for a short period. No load should be placed on this type of scaffold.

One caution is necessary, the wood used for any scaffolding should be of good variety and scaffolding should be made to carry the men and tools only and no other load should be placed on the same.

Ladders

Ladders made of wood and bamboos are most commonly used. Apart from these aluminum ladders are advantageously used in some places. For certain construction work rope ladders are conveniently used.

Wooden ladders made with suitable quality and sections of wood and standard width and 12 in rung to rung and coated with paint or varnish (to increase resistance of wood to decay) should only be used. These ladders should be inspected periodically and are with broken side rail and broken, loose or missing rung should be stocked properly on racks and not kept on the ground.

Bamboo ladders are aboused in construction sites but the author recommends that whenever such ladders are used extra safety measures should be taken.

Aluminum ladders are light, safe and convenient for use. A single person can with easily carry a 15 ft. aluminum ladder to place of work. Readymade aluminum ladders of different lengths are available. Though the initial cost is high, this is off set by their longer life. These ladders more over are stronger than wooden ladders will not decay, are more readily inspect and do not become tarnished when exposed to high room temperatures. Ladders made of magnesium alloy are still lighter than aluminum ones. The ladders may be cautioned against use of metallic ladders near exposed electrical equipments including overhead distribution wires, crane power rails, switch board etc.

Rope ladders should only be used where it is absolutely essential. The ropes should be at least 1 in. Sisal and rungs should be made of proper quality of wood. The wooden rungs should be placed 12 in. apart and tied properly with the rope. Each foot of the ladder and each rung should be inspected properly before use. The bottom end of the ladder should be fastened where possible to reduce swaying while climbing up or down. Not more than one person at a time should use the ladder.

There are certain rules to be followed in using a ladder. Firstly, the length of the ladder should be so chosen that the work can be performed from at least the fourth rung from the top of the ladder. Secondly, the ladder should be placed at such an angle that its foot is L/4 away from the object it is leaning against, where L is the length of the ladder.

Derricks

The term is usually applied to a fixed lifting device which utilizes some form of mast and imparts horizontal motion to the load only through mast or boom movement and rotation. Common types include: Gin pole, a frame, guy, stiff leg.

These are quite commonly used for construction work. The gin pole made of wood or steel pipe is popularly used in day to day maintenance and construction work and is a very simple and inexpensive device.

Cranes

Almost every where electric overhead traveling cranes are available for handling materials. These are handy and convenient for rigging work involved in maintenance and construction. Only one caution is necessary that the load should never exceed the specified capacity and no cross pulling should be done, but vertical lifts made.

Also cranes such as Wall crane, Gantry crane, one leg gantry crane and Gib crane are used in various places. This type is so constructed that the boom may be moved in vertical place, thus imparting translatory motion to the load hook, without raising or lowering the latter if the hoist drum is stationary. Such cranes are speedier and safer.

Then there are several mobile and truck cranes as follows:

- Truck crane
- Crawler crane
- Other mobile cranes as 'Hyster', 'Demag' etc. with non-rotating jib.
- Steam loco crane
- Diesel loco crane.

The important point to be noted in the use of the above cranes is the fact that the lifting capacity is a function of the radius. A 40 tonne crane may be able to lift only 5 tonnes at the maximum radius. Crane loading chart usually fixed on the crane should be referred to. Some cranes are provided with load and radius indicators which are very useful. In no case should the capacity at that radius be exceeded. With cranes as truck, steam loco and diesel loco, outriggers are provided which when used, higher loads can be lifted. These outriggers should be supported on hard ground and must be properly packed. In several accidents cranes have over turned due to snapping of slings attached to the load. It is necessary to use proper size slings and the slings should not be passed over sharp edges.

Hoists

Hand, electric and pneumatic hoists are very commonly used for mono-rails and jib cranes. Here again the capacity of the hoist should never be exceeded and no cross pull is allowed.

Winches

Hand, electrical, steam and pneumatic winches are commonly used in construction for hoisting and pulling. Generally, wire ropes and sometimes fiber ropes are used on drums. Snatch blocks are conveniently used with winches for changing direction of rope and with sheave blocks 2 to 6 parts rope could be employed to lift heavier loads.

Hoist Signals, Safety Belts, Accident Prevention

Hoist Signals

To reduce to the absolute minimum the number of accidents due to faulty or misunderstood signals when handling loads with cranes and hoists it is essential that only approved signals be used and these should be thoroughly understood by the signal man and the operator. The operator should take signals from only one authorized signalman and the practice of the several people signaling at a time should be condemned.

For derricks and special temporary hoists where the operator can not see the signal man, whistle signals as given below may be used.

To hoist	–	Two quick signals
To lower	–	Three quick signals
To stop	–	One quick signal
For emergency stop	–	Series of quick signals

For slow or cautious motion, use slower signals and hold the signal until it is desired to stop the motion.

Accident Prevention

The following are the safety rules for riggers:

1. Do not drop or throw things from an elevation.
2. Do not allow persons to walk below a suspended load or near slack cable which may suddenly be pulled out.
3. Do not wear loose clothing.
4. Wear hard hats and safety shoes.
5. Wear safety belts when working at heights above 12 ft. from ground. The tail line should be as short as practicable and it should be fastened to a rigid member above the man's waist.
6. Wear safety goggles where there is a hazard to eyes due to dust or flying particles.
7. Do not leave bolts, tools, slings and other equipment lying on beams or other supports where they can become dislodged and fall on to passers by.
8. When two slings are required to be used for lifting and load the angle with the horizontal should not be

less than 30° in any case, as there are all the chances of the slings coming off the hook with any lesser angle.

9. Wire rope and manila rope used on any job should be thoroughly inspected before use; as also ladders, pulley blocks, safety belts scaffolding and all other materials used by a rigger.

10. Before lifting any load manually estimate its weight and be sure that it is not too heavy to lift. Get your feet on a good flat surface where they will not slip and as close to the object as possible. Then squat down bending the knees but keeping the back straight. Get a good firm grip on the object and holding it close to the body lift with leg muscles.

    To place back the load on the floor, reverse the above procedure keeping the back straight, bend the knees and carefully lower the object until one corner or edge touches the floor then carefully remove your fingers and allow the other side of the object to rest on the floor. Be careful of your hand and fingers while fixing slings on to a crane or hoist hook and while signaling to the operator to hoist. Such injuries are very common.

11. Never ride on crane hooks or on loads being handled by a crane or hoist.

12. Only one authorized person should signal to a crane operator and standard signals understood by both should be used.

13. Never leave scaffolding hanging after the work is over. It is likely to be used at a later date by some other party who is liable to meet with an accident due to decayed parts of the scaffolding.

14. Never place any load on scaffoldings which are meant to carry only men and tools.

15. Never overload jacks, chain blocks, chain pullers, cranes, slings, wire rope, fiber rope, shackles etc. It is a good practice to use tackles with 25% higher capacity than the load to be lifted. It should be mentioned here that the weight of the material to be lifted should be estimated correctly. Do not guess.
16. Slings should never be passed over sharp edges of the load. Use wooden blocks, gunny bag padding or half round pipe to avoid damage to sling and subsequent falling of the load.
17. All injuries however slight should be reported and first aid treatment given at once in order to avoid infections and other complications at a later date.

Rollers

Heavy or bulky objects often moved on the rollers. Main hazard is fingers or toes getting pinched or crushed between the roller and the floor or the roller and the object, when the direction of the roller is changed.

To move a roller under load, use a sledge or a bar; never hand or foot.

Crowbars

Whenever a crowbar is needed, the proper size and kind of bar for the job should be used. Make shifts such as a piece of pipe or an iron bar should never be substituted for a crowbar, since they may slip and cause injury.

The crowbar should have a point or toe of such shape that it will grip the object to be moved, and a heel to act as a pivot or fulcrum. In some cases, a block of wood under the heel will prevent the crowbar from slipping and injuring the hand.

Crowbars not in use should be stood on end so that they will not fall, or laid on the ground where they will not create a stumbling hazard.

Weights of Common Materials

Material	Lbs. per Cu.ft.	Kg. per m^3
Aluminum	165	2440
Brass	534	8550
Bronze, Phosphor	554	8870
Copper	556	8910
Iron (Cast)	450	7210
Lead	710	11380
Steel	487	7810
Tin	459	7360
Zinc	440	7050
Cork	15	240.5
Glass, plate	162	2595
Leather	59	945
Rubber goods	94	1515
Wood, Teak	48	770
Wood, Oak-Red	42	673
Wood, pine	34	545
Wood, walnut	37	593
Oil, Mineral, Lubricants	57	914
Water (4°C)	62.428	1000.0
Ice	56	897.0
Brick Masonry (Red brick)	112	1794
Concrete Masonry (cement, stone, sand)	144	2308
Earth, dry loose	76	1218
Earth, Moist, packed	96	1540
Sand, Gravel, Dry, Loose	90-105	1440-1682
Sand, Gravel, Wet	126	2020
Asbestos	153	2450
Lose stone quarried	95	1523
Coal, piled	47-58	754-930
Coke, piled	23-32	318-513.

FIGURES AND TABLES ON SAFE RIGGING PRACTICE

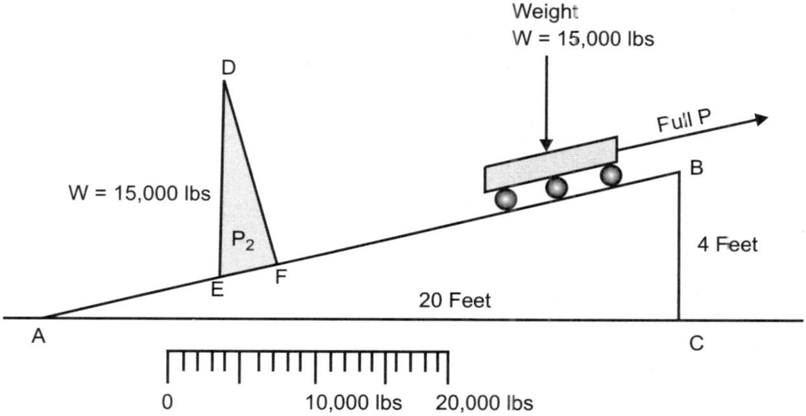

Fig. 1: Inclined Plane.

Fig. 1 shows the inclined plane. If a load of 15,000 lbs. is required to be pulled up an inclined of 1 foot in 5 feet on rollers the pull P required can be easily figured out by drawing a vector diagram DEF where DE represents the load (15,000 lbs.) and EF is proportional to the pull. This works out to be approximately 3,000 lbs. This is theoretical and rollers have been supposed to be frictionless.

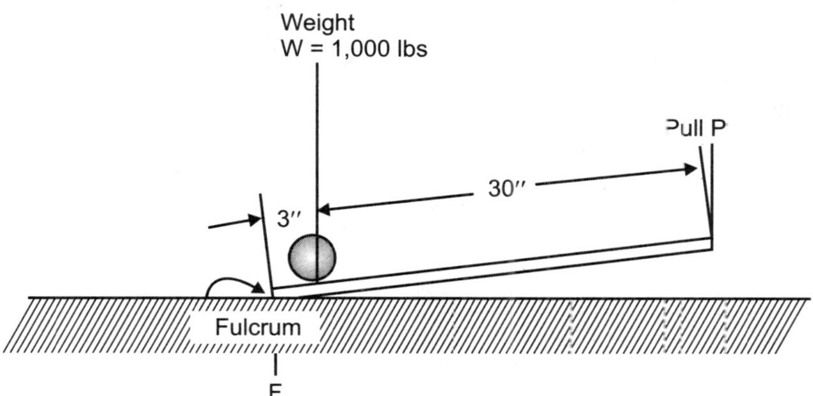

(a)

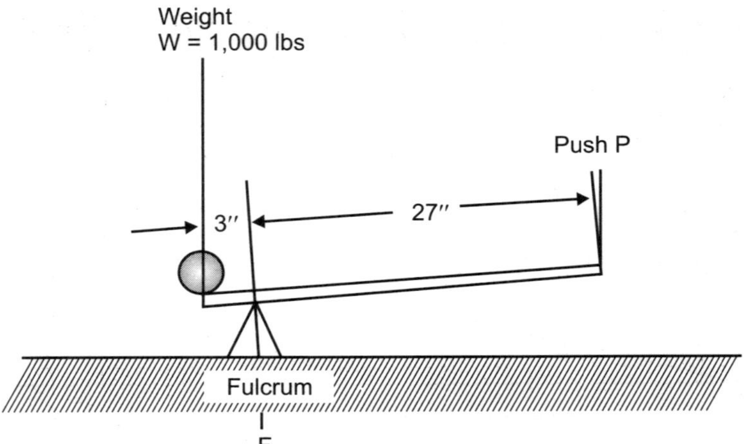

(b)

Fig. 2: Crow-Bar.

Fig. 2 shows the advantage gained by using a crow-bar which is typical lever. In Fig. 2 (a) the pull P required to lift a weight of 1000 lbs. is 1000 × 3/30 or 100 lbs. and in (b), the pull P is 1000 × 3/27 or 111 lbs, so the crow-bar most efficient, or less force is required when used as in a.

Table 1: Safe working loads for fibre rope falls

Rope Diameter	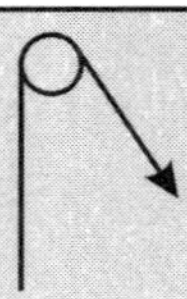	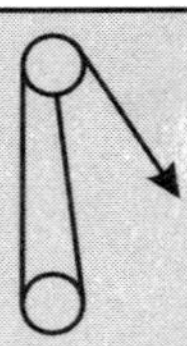	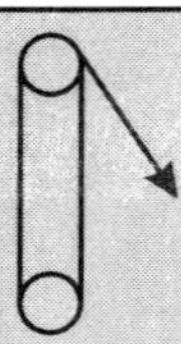	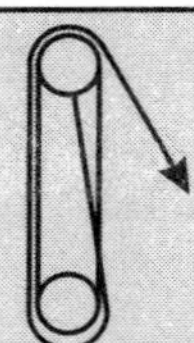
Inches	1 Part	2 Part	3 Part	4 Part
	Tons	Tons	Tons	Tons
1/2	0.11	0.20	0.27	0.32
3/4	0.22	0.40	0.54	0.66
1	0.37	0.67	0.91	1.00

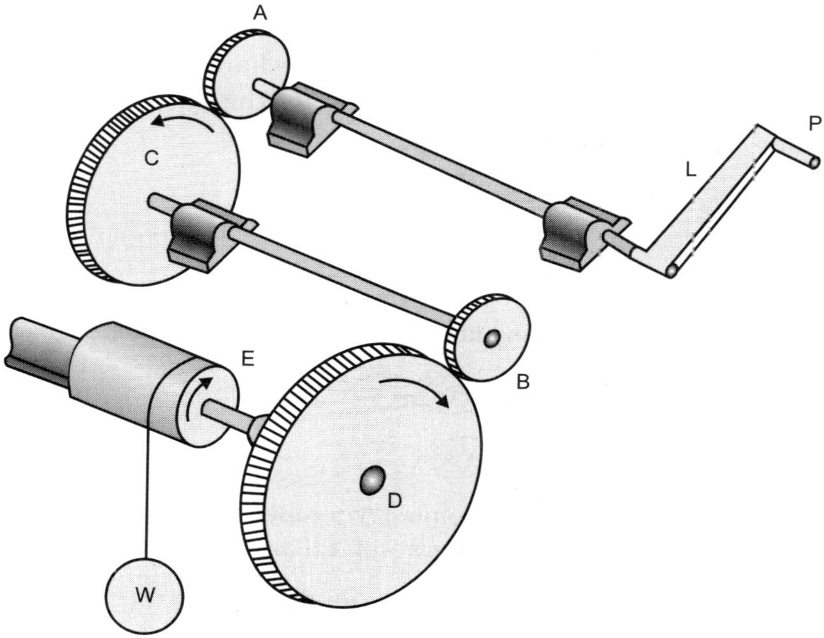

Fig. 3: Winch with a train of gears.

A typical winch with a train of gears to get mechanical advantage is shown in Fig. 3. The theoretical force P required to hoist a load W is:

$$P = \frac{W \times E \times A \times B}{L \times C \times D}$$

where,

P = Force on lever or crank, lb.

E = Radius of drum, to centre of rope, in.

W = Weight to be lifted, lb.

L = Length of hand crank or lever, in.

A = No. of teeth of position A

B = No. of teeth of position B

C = No. of teeth of gear C

D = No. of teeth of gear D

The general knowledge of these mechanical movements will help the rigger to understand better the operation of the tools and machines that he uses in his work.

Fig. 4 (a): Granny knot. May slip or jam. Unsafe.

Fig. 4 (b): Reef knot. For joining two ropes of same size, will not hold if ropes are wet. Efficiency 50%.

Fig. 4 (c): Two half hitches. For attaching rope to ring.

Fig. 4 (d): Anchor knot. For eastening rope to post.

Fig. 4 (e): Bowline A slipping eye. Will not jam. Easily untied. Efficiency 60%.

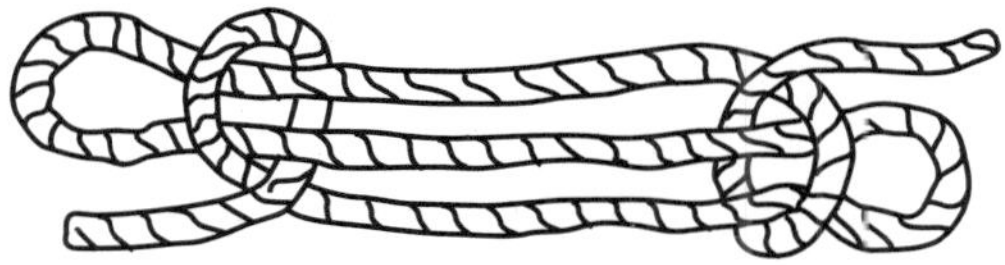

Fig. 4 (f): Sheepshank. For shortening a rope without cutting it.

Fig. 4 (g): Backwal hitch.
For temporarily attaching a rope to a hook.

Fig. 4 (h): Double backwall hitch.
Will not slip even if rope is wet or greasy.

Fig. 4 (i): Timber hitch. For hoisting or hauling poles and pipes.

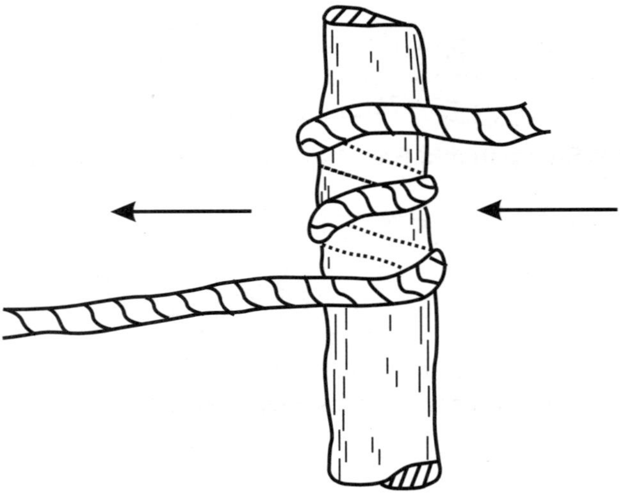

Fig. 4 (j): Snubber. For holding or slowly lowering a heavy load.

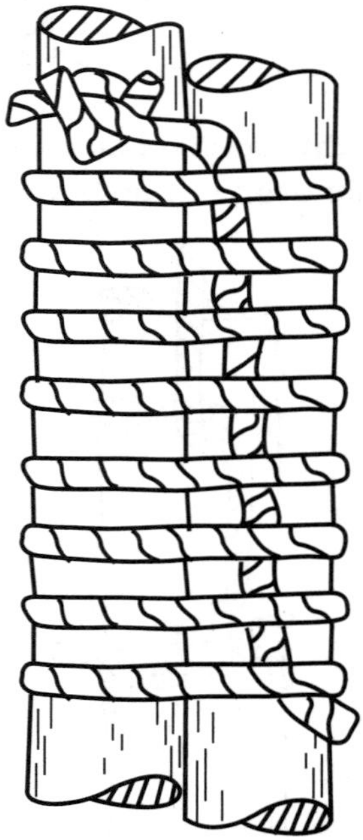

Fig. 4 (k): Poles lashing. For lashing poles together, two such lashing should be used.

Fig. 4 (l): Scaffold hitch.
For suspending a scaffold plank from tilting.

Fig. 4 (m): Barrel hitch vertical. For hosting a barrel or similar object. Tie rope as shown, then pull parts as indicates by arrows.

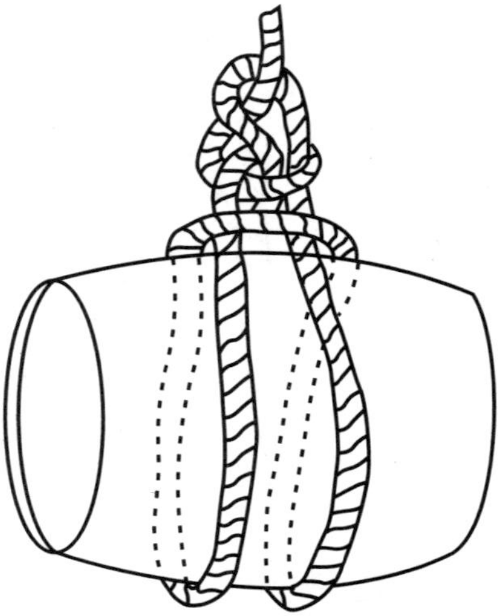

Fig. 4 (n): Barrel hitch horizontal.

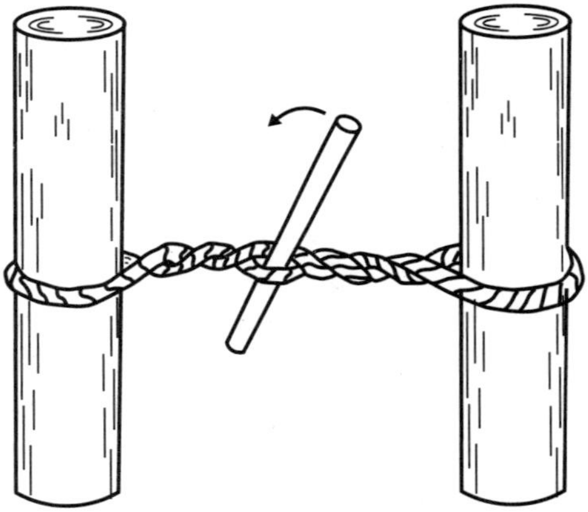

Fig. 4 (o): Spanish swindlers.

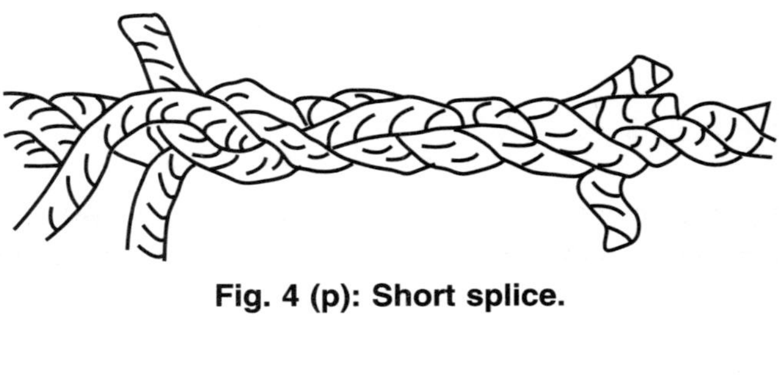

Fig. 4 (p): Short splice.

Fig. 4 (q): Eye splice.

Fig. 4 (r): Whipping.

(1) Right lay, regular lay wire rope

(2) Alternate lay wire rope

(3) Left lay, regular lay wire rope

(4) Long lay, long lay wire rope.

Fig. 5: Four different ways of laying the wire rope.

Table 2: Common use of various construction of wire ropes

6 × 7 Regular lay.		Guys, suspension ropes etc.
6 × 19 Regular lay with hemp core.		Slings tackle-blocks clampshell, buckets, elevator.
6 × 19 Regular lay with steel core.	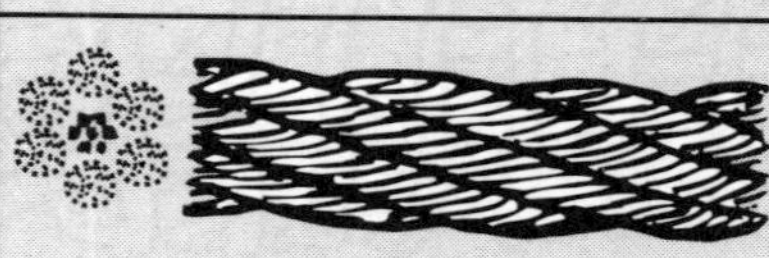	Hot beds blast furnace bell hoist etc.
6 × 37 Regular lay with hemp core.	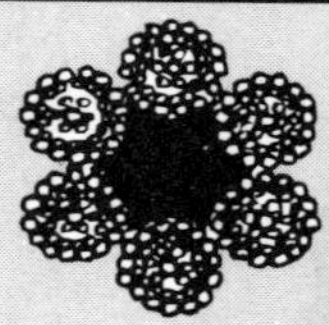	Overhead cranes, mill hoist etc.
6 × 37 Regular lay with steel core.		Hot metals cranes, pit side casting cranes, Blast furnace bell and skip hoist etc.
Lacked coil.	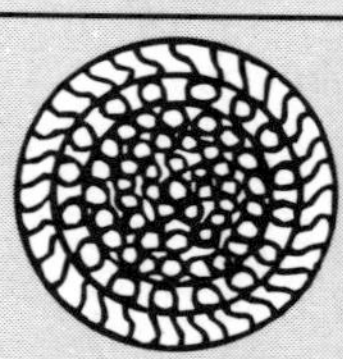	Blast furnace gauge rod.

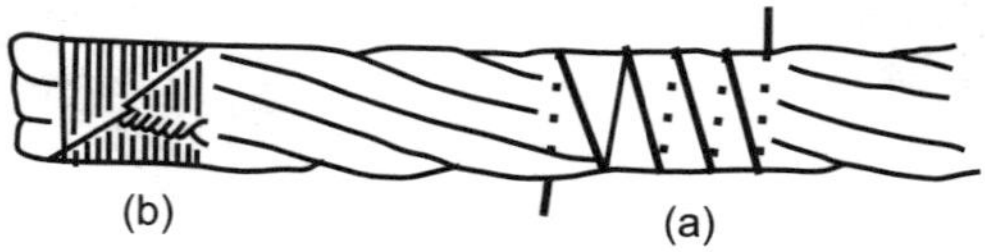

Fig. 6: At (a) the turns of the seizing wire are spread apart to illustrate method of applying them. Completed seizing is shown at (b).

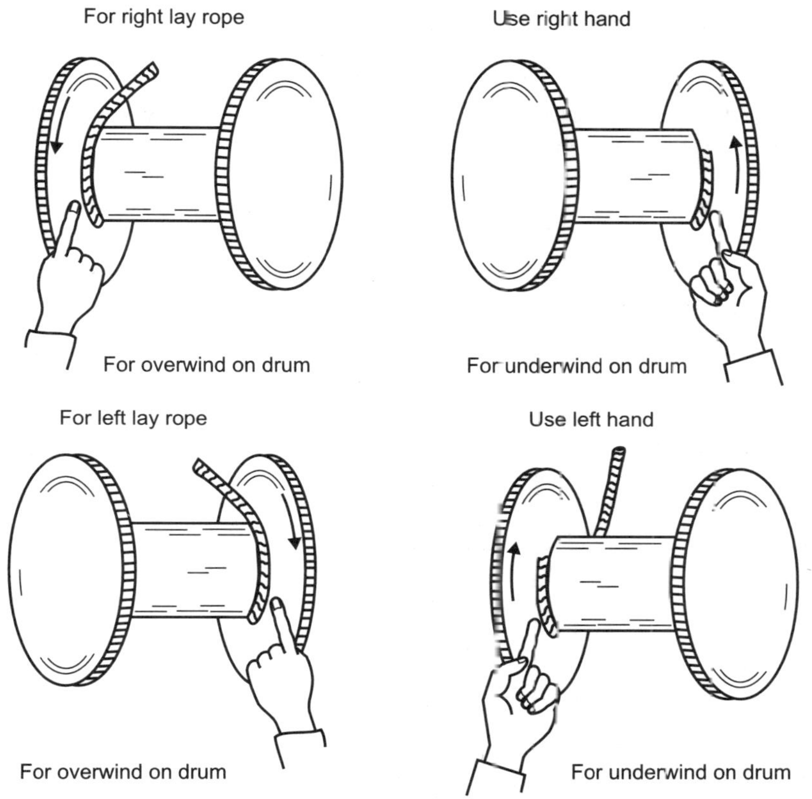

Fig. 7

Fig. 8 (a) and (b)

Table 3: Number of clips and spacing for safe application

Rope diam. (in.)	Approx. weight (lb.)	Minimum No. of clips for each rope end	Spacing* of clips (in.)
3/16	0.10	2	1.1/8
1/4	.10	2	1.1/2
5/16	.29	2	1.7/8
3/8	.47	2	2.1/4
7/16	.70	2	2.5/8
1/2	.78	3	3
5/8	1.06	3	3.1/4
3/4	1.59	4	4.1/2
7/8	2.40	4	5.1/4
1	2.72	4	6
1.2/8	3.20	5	6.3/4
1.1/4	4.50	5	7.1/2
1.3/8	4.60	6	8.1/4
1.1/2	5.80	6	9
1.3/8	7.20	6	9.1/4
1.1/4	9.50	7	10.1/2
2	12.50	8	12
2.1/4	15.50	8	13.1/2
2.1/2	18.00	8	15
Clips furnished in drop-forged steel, Galvanized steel, or cast-steel base, as specified.			

*Centre to centre of U-bolts.

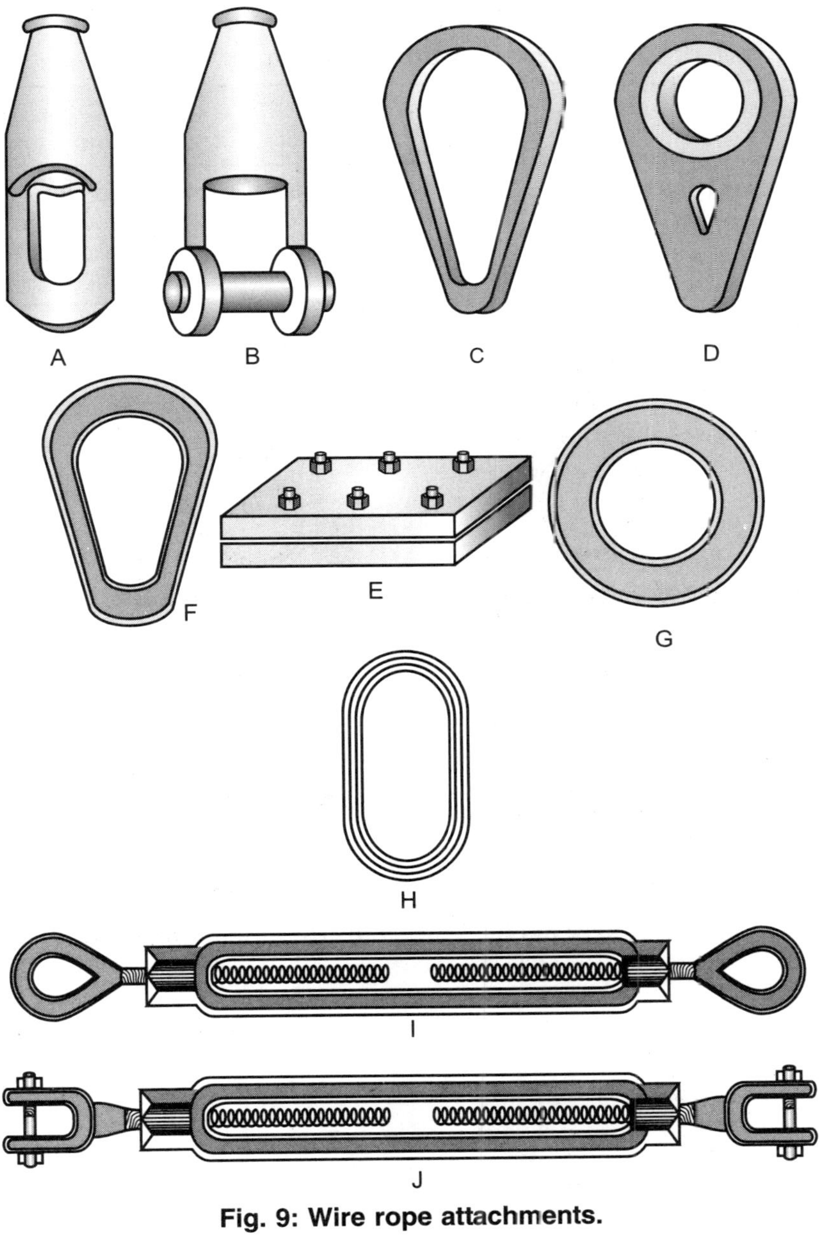

Fig. 9: Wire rope attachments.

Table 4: Allowable wire breaks and wear on hoisting ropes

Use	Conditions	6 × 19 core	6 × 37	8 × 19 core	6 × 19 scale	Other conditions
Cranes	Total Adjacent		18	30	24	Wear on outside wires in excess of 33%
	Adjacent		4	6	4	
Hoists	Total Adjacent		24	.....		
			5	.....		

Fig. 10: Endless sling.

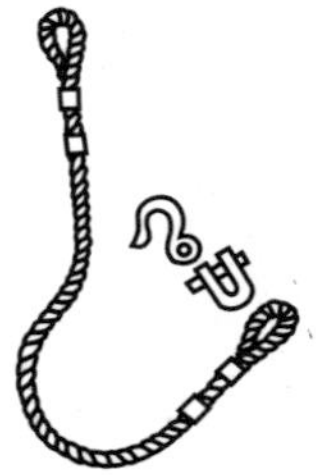

Fig. 11: Single sling.

Fig. 12: Basket hitch.

Fig. 13: Single choker sling.

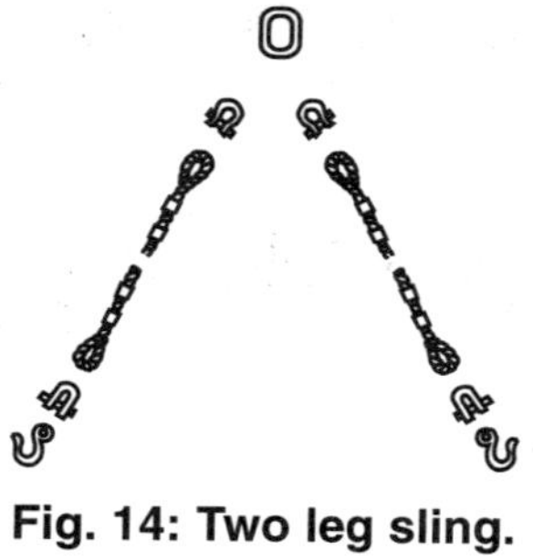

Fig. 14: Two leg sling.

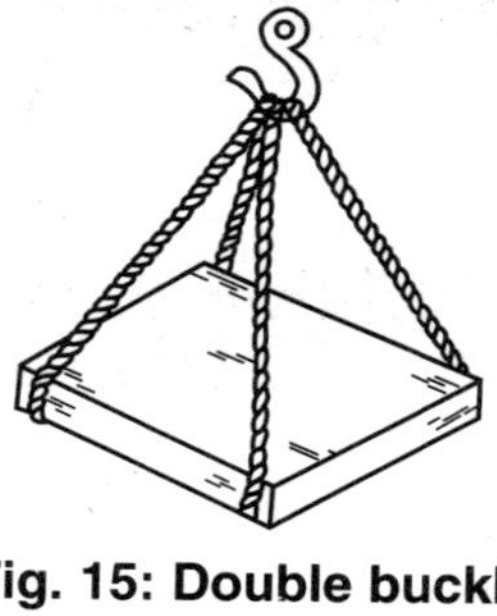

Fig. 15: Double buckle sling.

Fig. 16: Double chocker sling.

Fig. 17: The bridle sling.

Fig. 18: Four-leg bridle sling with spliced eyes.

Table 5 (a): Safe working loads for wire rope slings

	One leg	Choker One leg	Choker Two leg	Choker Two leg	Choker Two leg	U sling
Wire rope diameter			60°	45°	30°	
Inches	Tons	Tons	Tons	Tons	Tons	Tons
1/4	0.4	0.3	0.5	0.4	0.3	0.8
3/8	0.9	0.6	1.1	0.9	0.6	1.7
1/2	0.5	1.1	1.9	1.6	1.1	3.0
5/8	2.3	1.7	3.0	2.4	1.7	4.6
3/4	3.4	2.6	4.4	3.4	2.6	6.8
7/8	4.3	3.2	5.6	6.6	3.2	8.6
1	5.7	4.2	7.3	6.0	4.2	11.3
1.1/4	8.7	6.5	11.2	9.1	6.4	17.3

Table 5 (b): Safe working loads for rope slings

	Basket	Basket	Basket	Two Leg	Two Leg	Two Leg
Wire rope diameter	60°	45°	30°	60°	45°	30°
Inches	Tons	Tons	Tons	Tons	Tons	Tons
1/4	0.5	0.4	0.3	0.7	0.6	0.4
3/8	1.1	0.9	0.6	1.5	1.2	0.9
1/2	1.9	1.6	1.1	2.6	2.1	1.5
5/8	3.0	2.4	1.7	4.0	3.3	2.3
3/4	4.4	3.6	2.6	5.9	4.8	3.4
7/8	5.6	4.6	3.2	7.5	6.1	4.3
1	7.3	6.0	4.2	9.8	8.0	5.7
1.1/4	11.2	9.1	6.4	14.9	12.2	8.7

(a)

(b)

Fig. 19: (a) Six-part flat-braided sling; (b) Eight-part round-braided sling.

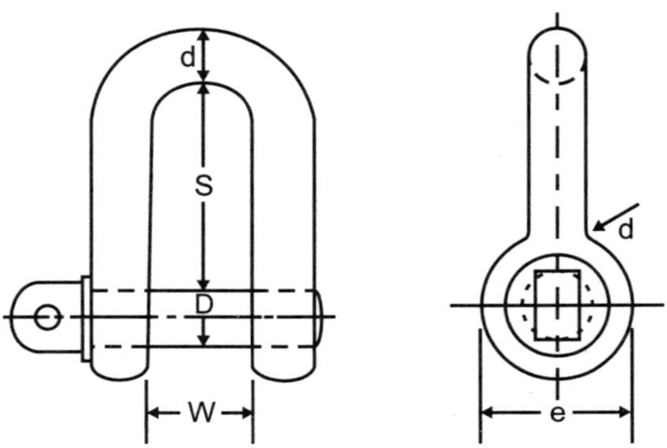

Fig. 20(a): 'D' type shackle.

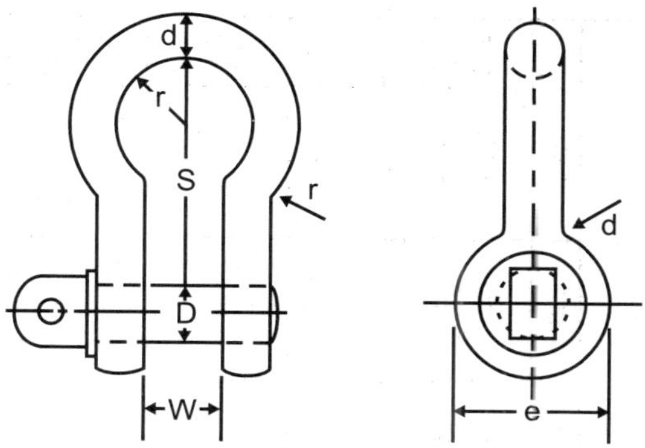

Fig. 20(b): 'Bow' type shackle.

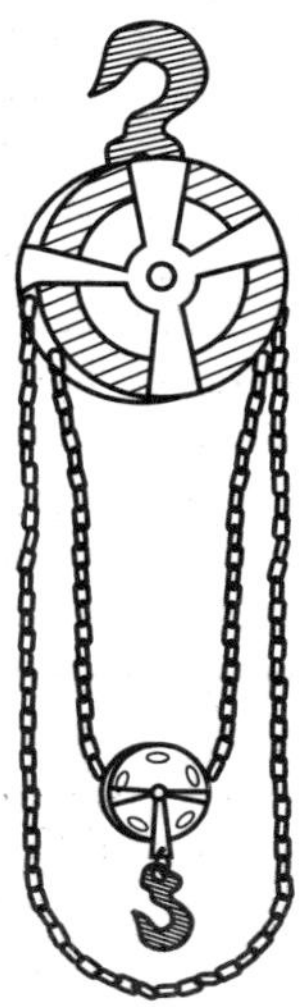

Fig. 22: Chain hoists.

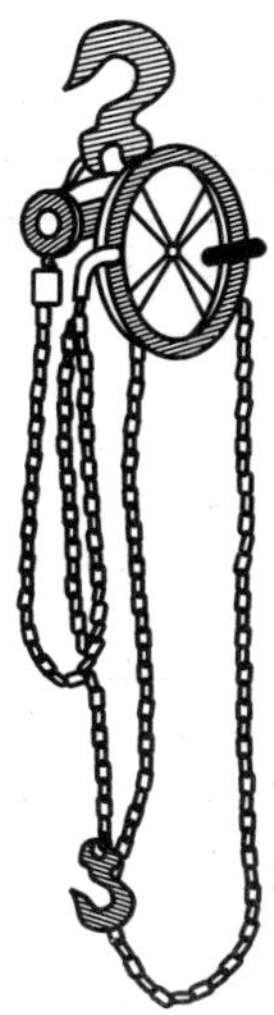

Fig. 21.

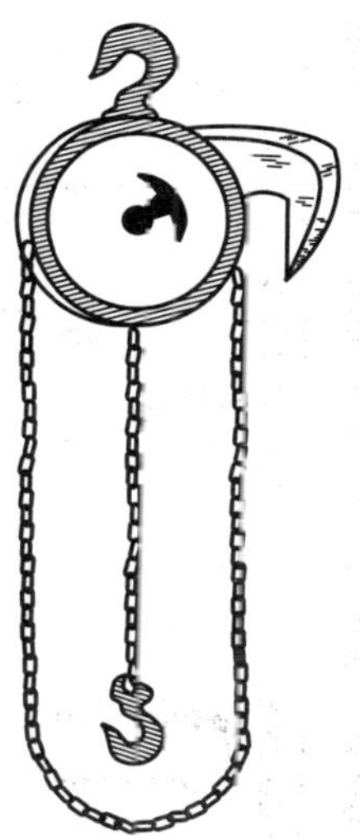

Fig. 23.

Table 6: Safe working loads for sling chains

Single Sling / Slip or Collar Sling					Endless sling				Double sling				Load Evenly Don't Overload Read Tables Carefully								
													30°		60°		90°		120°		
Dia of Chain	Test load admibality		Maximum working load		Test load on the double chain		Maximum working load on double		Test load on the double sling		Maximum working load double										Dia of Chain
Inches	Tons	Cwts.	Tons	Cwts.	Tons	Cwts.	Tons	Cwts.	Tons	Cwts.	Tons	Cwts.	Tons	Cwts.	Tons	Cwts.	Tons	Cwts.	Tons	Cwts.	Inches
1/4		15		7	1	10		15	1	10		15		14		13		10		7	1/4
5/16	1	2		11	2	4	1	2	2	4	1	2	1	2		19		16		11	5/16
3/8	1	12		16	3	4	1	12	3	4	1	12	1	11	1	8	1	3		16	3/8
7/16	2	5	1	2	4	10	2	5	4	10	2	5	2	3	1	19	1	12	1	2	7/16
1/2	3	0	1	10	6	0	3	0	6	0	3	0	2	18	2	12	2	2	1	10	1/2
9/16	3	15	1	17	7	10	3	15	7	10	3	15	3	12	3	5	2	13	1	17	9/16
5/8	4	12	2	6	9	4	4	12	9	4	4	12	4	9	4	0	3	5	2	6	5/8
11/16	5	12	2	16	11	4	5	12	11	4	5	12	5	9	4	17	4	0	2	16	11/16
3/4	6	15	3	7	13	10	6	15	13	10	6	15	6	10	5	17	4	15	3	7	3/4
7/8	9	2	4	11	18	4	9	2	18	4	9	2	8	16	7	18	6	9	4	11	7/8
1	12	0	6	0	24	0	12	0	24	0	12	0	11	12	10	8	8	10	6	0	1
1⅛	15	2	7	11	30	4	15	2	30	4	15	2	14	12	13	2	10	14	7	11	1⅛
1¼	18	15	9	7	37	10	18	15	37	10	18	15	18	2	16	9	13	5	9	7	1¼
1⅜	22	12	11	6	45	4	22	12	45	4	22	12	21	17	19	12	16	0	11	6	1⅜
1½	27	0	13	10	54	0	27	0	54	0	27	0	26	1	23	18	19	2	13	10	1½

Fig. 24: Screw jack with ratchet handle.

Fig. 25: Journal jack.

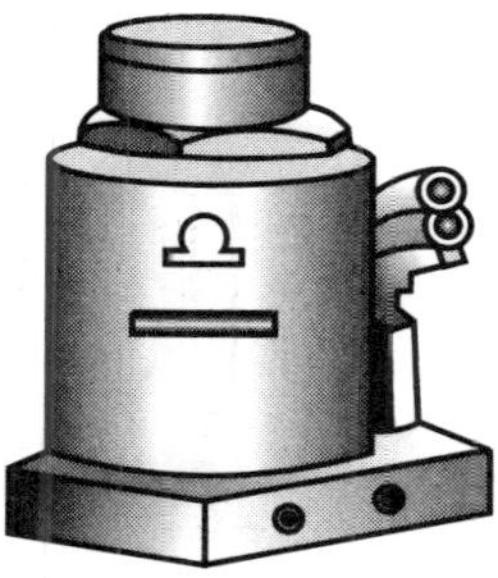

Fig. 26: Hydraulic jack with built in pump.

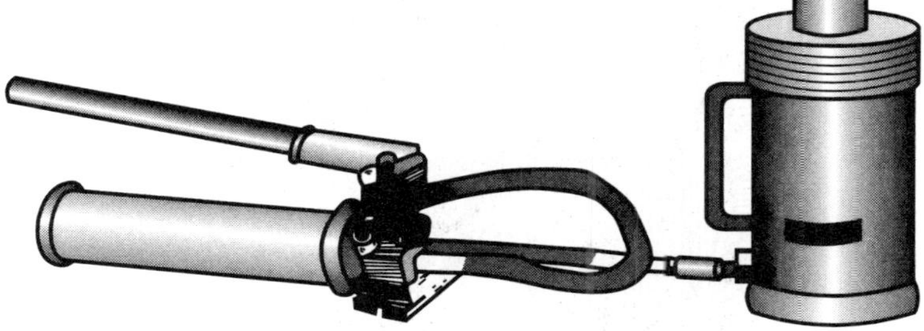

Fig. 27: Hydraulic jack with separate pump unit consists of hydraulic pump high pressure base, high pressure quick coupling and ram.

Fig. 28: Traveling jack.

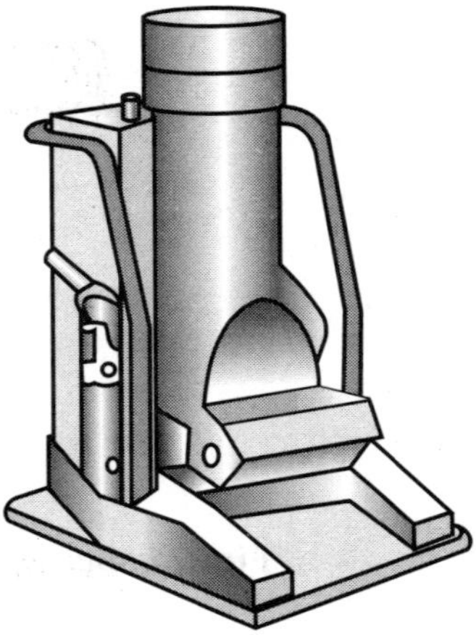

Fig. 29: Foot lift or Toe jack.

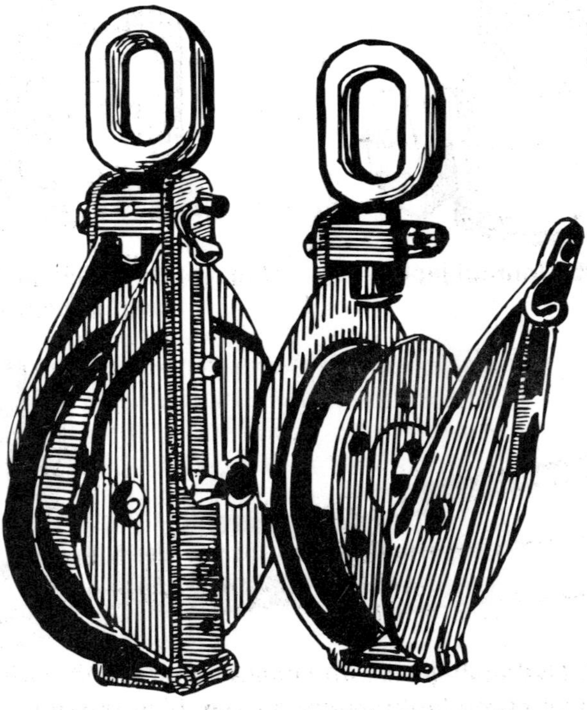

Fig. 30: Standard snatch-block with swivel oval eye.

Table 7: Safe working loads for rope falls

Wire rope diameter	Min. Dia. of sheave	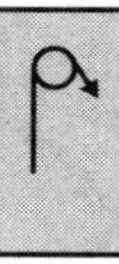		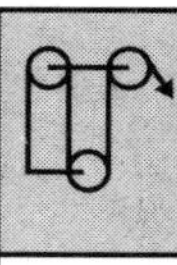	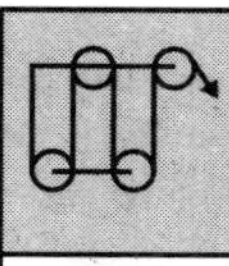	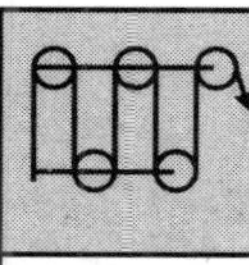	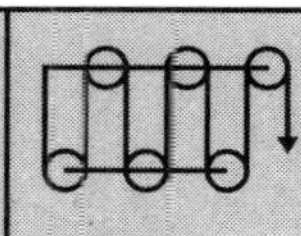
Inch	Inch	Tons	Tons	Tons	Tons	Tons	Tons
1/2	8	1.5	2.9	4.1	5.3	6.1	7.0
5/8	10	2.3	4.4	6.3	8.1	9.5	10.9
3/4	13	3.4	6.6	9.3	12.0	14.0	16.2
7/8	14	4.3	8.3	12.2	15.2	17.7	20.4
1	16	5.6	10.9	16.0	19.9	23.2	26.7

Fig. 31: Partially Fabricated Steel Scaffolding.

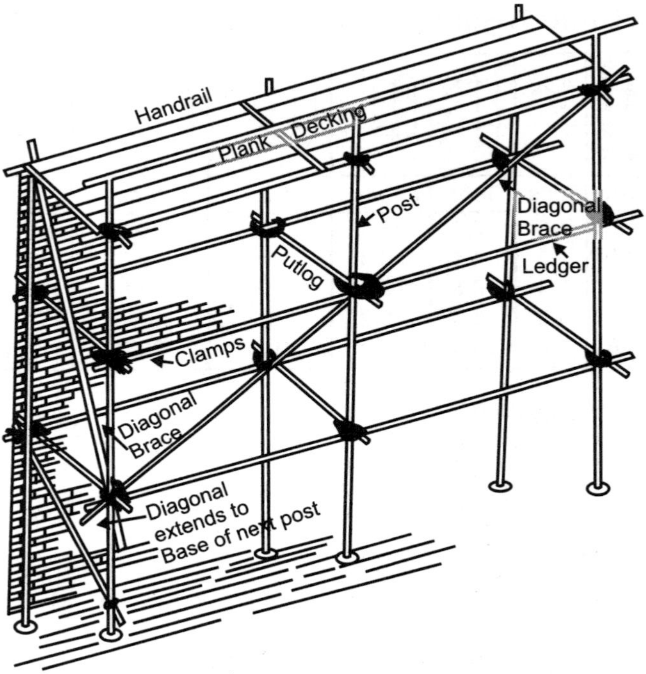

Fig. 32 (a): Tubular Steel Scaffolding.

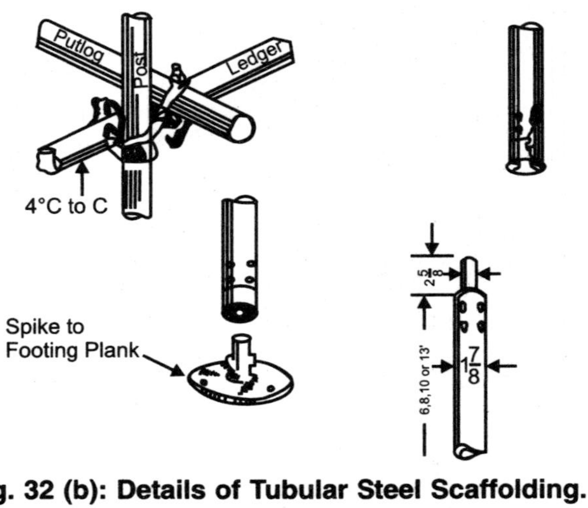

Fig. 32 (b): Details of Tubular Steel Scaffolding.

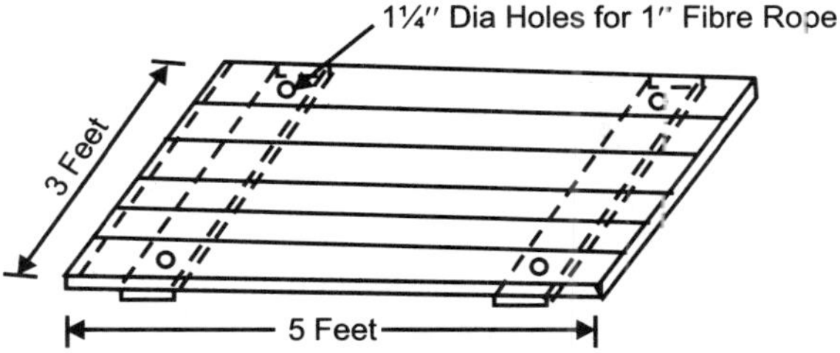

Fig. 33: Temporary Wooden Scaffold.

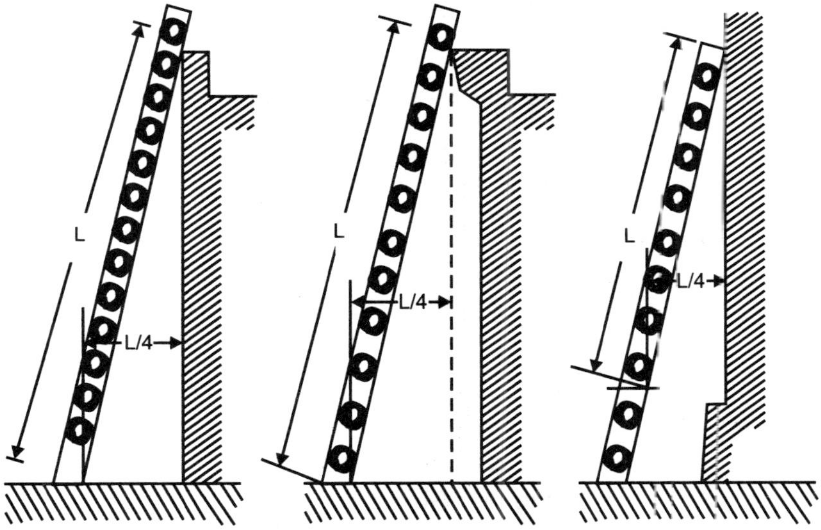

Fig. 34: Rules for Placing a Ladder at a Proper Angle.

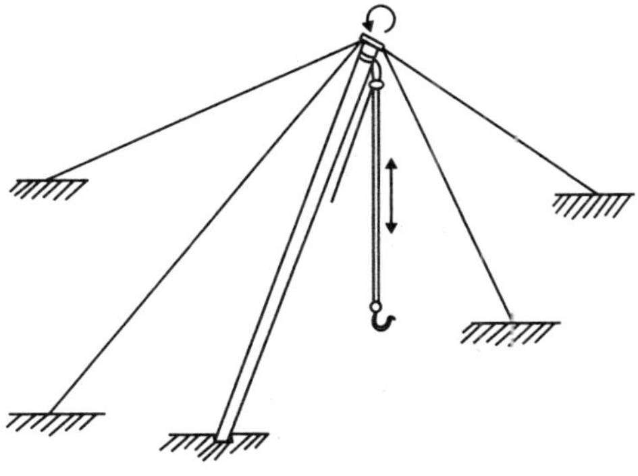

Fig. 35: Gin Pole.

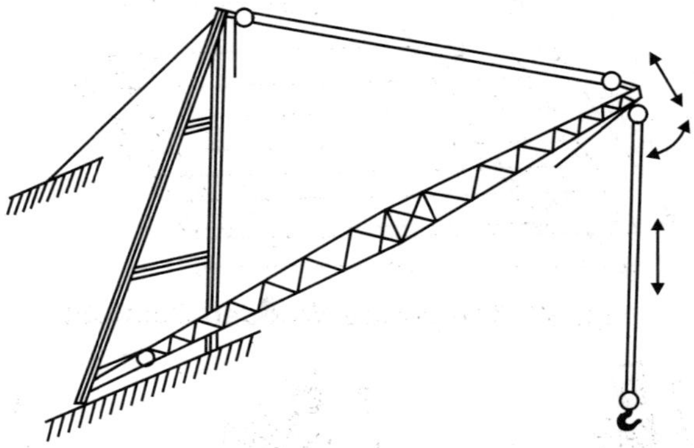

Fig. 36: A Frame Derrick.

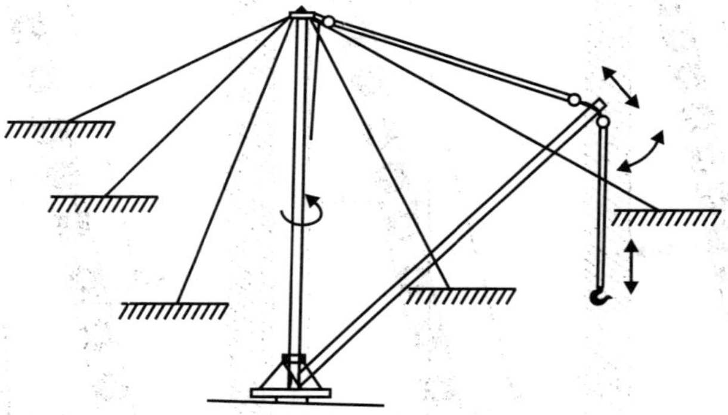

Fig. 37: Guyed Derrick.

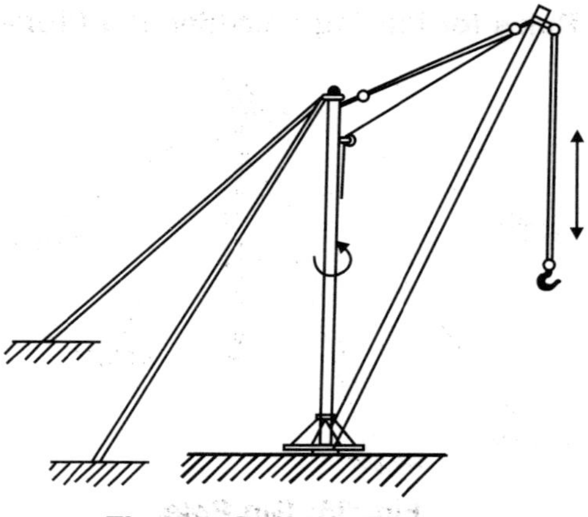

Fig. 38: Stiff-leg Derrick.

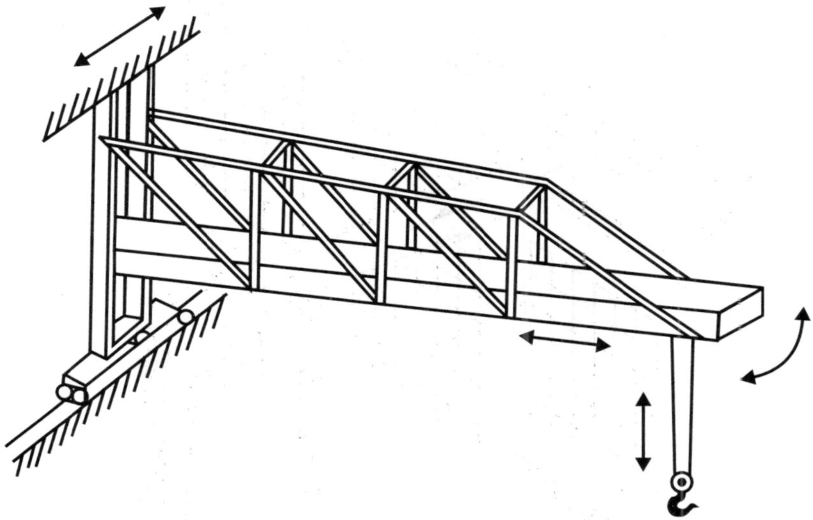

Fig. 39: Wall Crane.

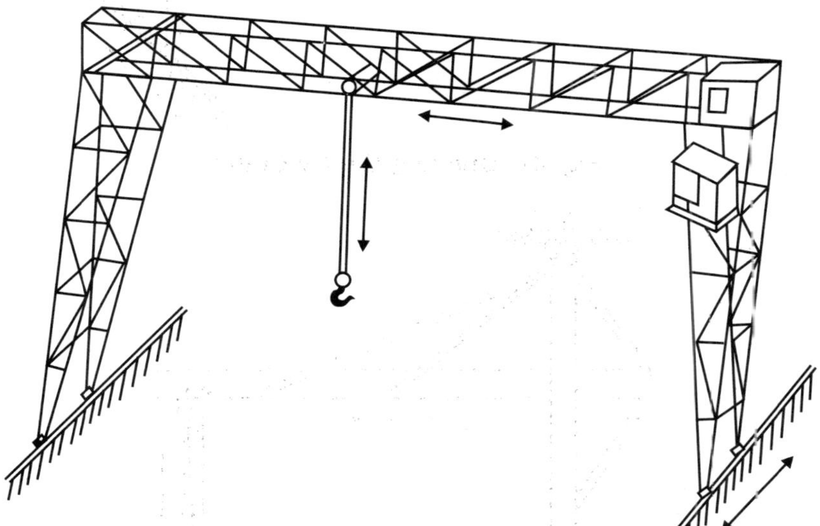

Fig. 40: Gantry Crane.

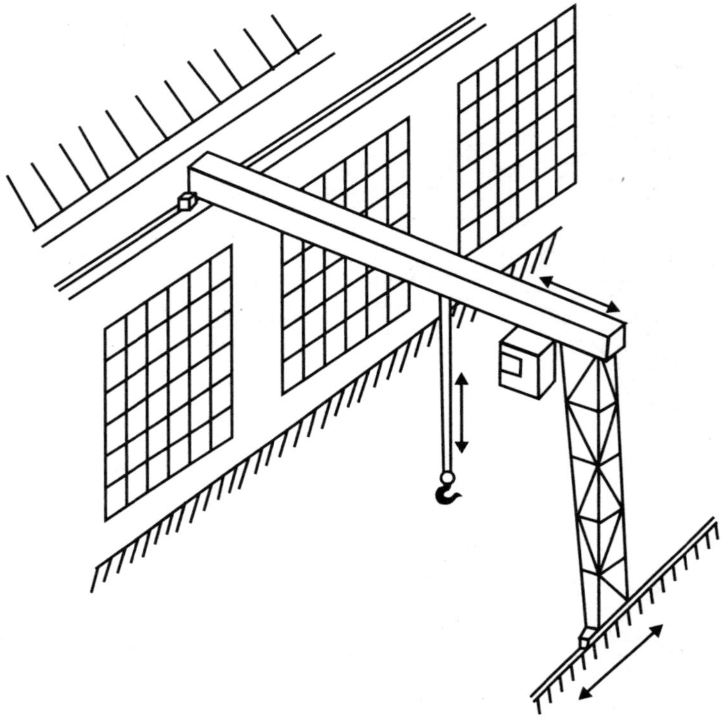

Fig. 41: One Leg Gantry Crane.

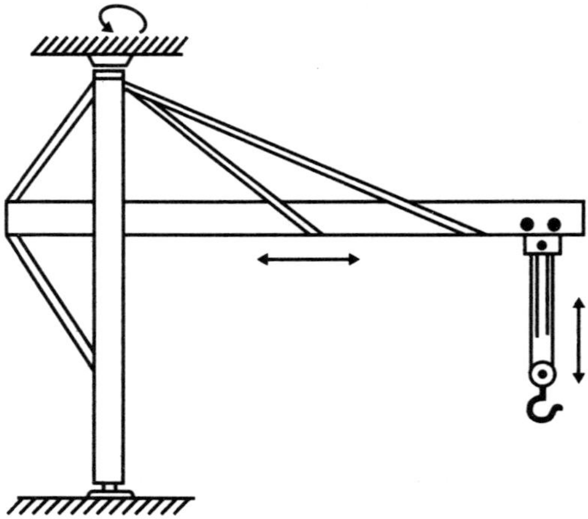

Fig. 42: Jib Crane.

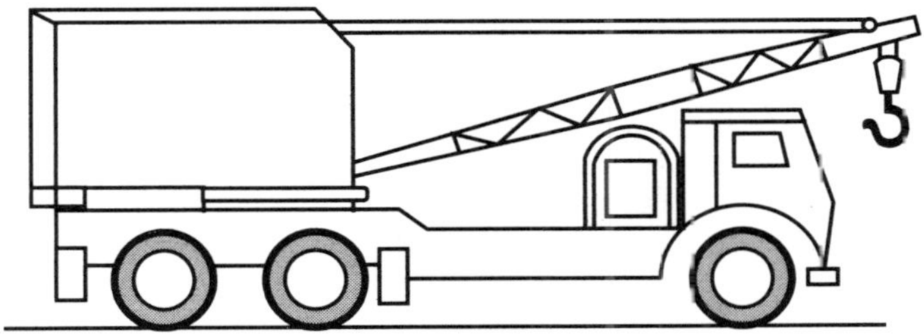

Fig. 43: Truck Crane.

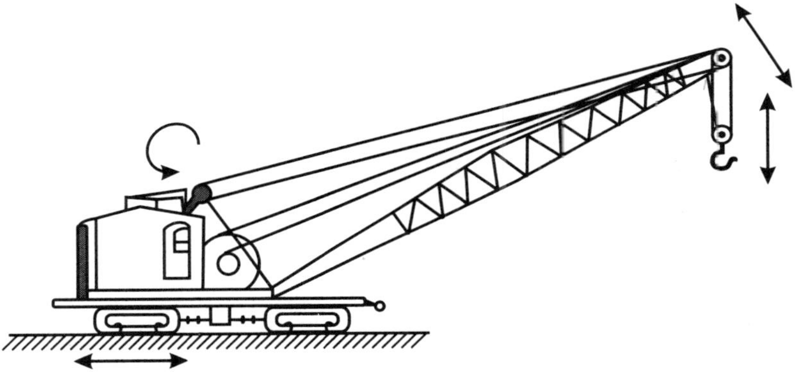

Fig. 44: Disel Loco Crane.

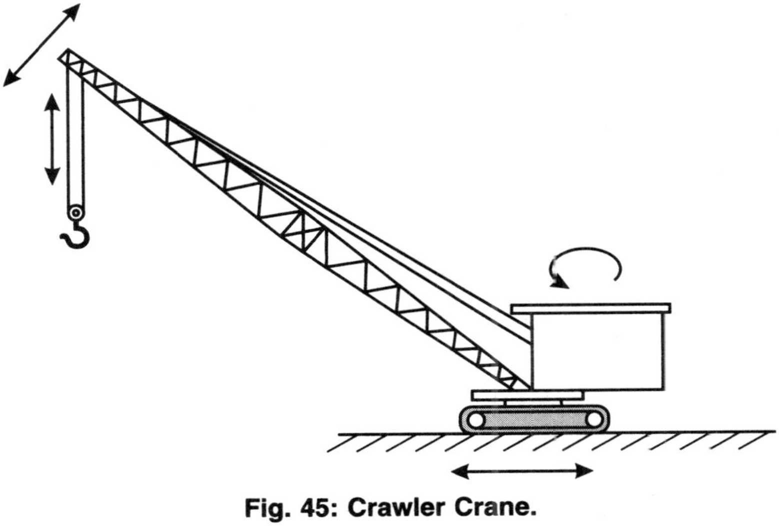

Fig. 45: Crawler Crane.

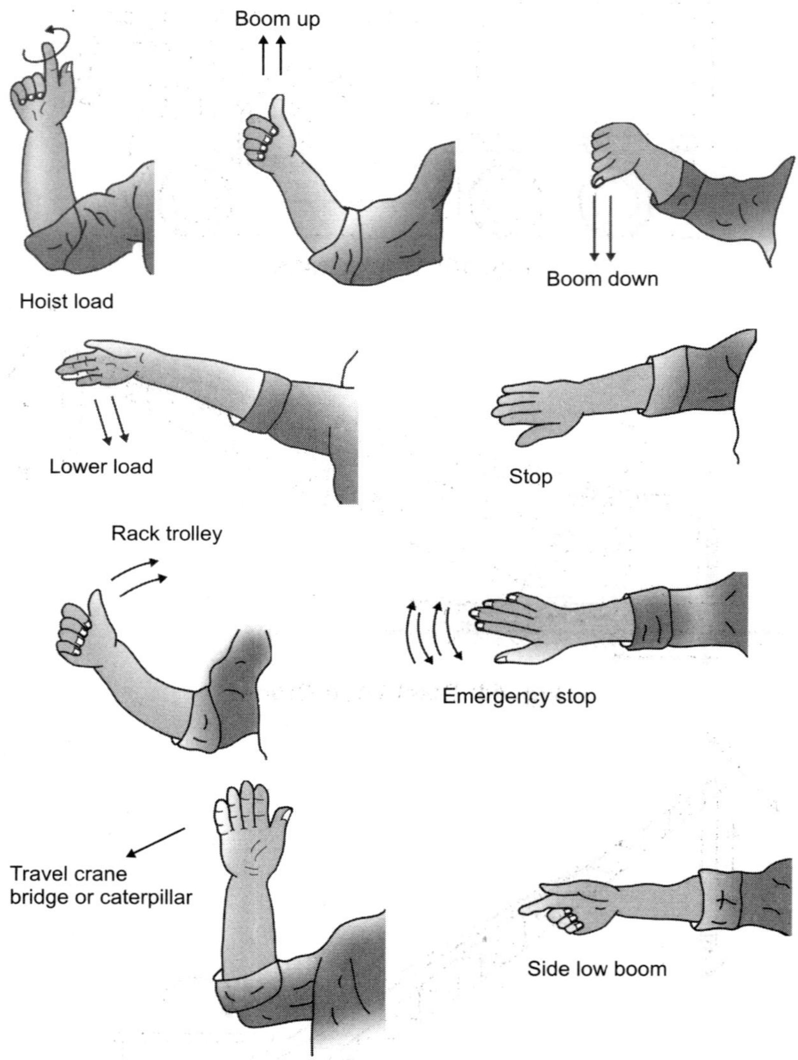

Fig. 46: Standard Crane Signals.

❒ ❒ ❒

CHAPTER 10

Construction Safety Rules

INTRODUCTION

Let us discuss on the construction safety rules as this will help in building awareness and guiding all to work more safely to stop the occurrence of accidents. The construction industry is one of the oldest and hazardous industries contributing to the major chunk of serious accidents. The construction workers must always be mindful on their job, failure to do so call for serious injury to them or to their fellow workers. Protective equipments differ from job to job; however, the basic equipments like safety helmets, safety glasses, safety shoes, and hand gloves are common and must be worn by all of them. Construction workers must save them from dehydration and plenty of drinking water facility must be provided to them also the workers know the location of water to utilize it in case of fire or a chemical burn. The improvement of good house keeping in construction site is a must to avoid unwanted accidents and to increase work efficiency. Construction workers must always be alert of sharp objects, such as nails and protruding objects. Construction workers training is essential prior to engage them into a job. This includes operators of all power tools and those of heavy machinery. Only the licensed drivers of heavy machinery should ride the vehicle. People who are working on the ground near heavy vehicle must be sure that driver is well aware of them. No machinery should be oiled, fueled and adjusted during running condition. There are many rules made to protect the construction workers working above the ground. The persons who are afraid of working at height must be segregated immediately after medical examination. Ladders and scaffolds used in construction must be made as per specification set by manufacturers.

THE GENERAL SAFETY RULES FOR CONSTRUCTION WORKERS

1. Always be mindful on your job. No horseplay should be done while on job.
2. Always wear all the personal protective equipment for the job.
3. Protect and prevent yourself from hot materials.
4. In case of contact with acid like substances immediately wash it with plenty of water.
5. Behave properly, walk properly; do not run in construction site.
6. The use of drugs and alcohol is strictly prohibited in construction site as these are the causes of many serious accidents. If you use some strong medicine with the advice of doctors, then it should be known to your immediate supervisor, so that he can allot you the jobs accordingly.

7. Do not try to attract the attention of others while doing the job.
8. Sanitation facilities are provided for you and for your colleagues. Try to keep it clean as far as it is possible. Do not try to deface or degrade or damage these facilities. These are forbidden acts and try to keep away from such jobs.
9. Cleanliness is the next to Godliness also clean job is the start of a safe job. Develop the habit of good house keeping.
10. Compressor air is the most costly form of energy and it also contains moisture and dirt etc. So do not use compressed air for the removal of dust from your clothes and from your body. This may seriously harm you.
11. Do not work at height if you are afraid to do so, also if you feel dizziness, nausea, and vomiting tendency then it is better to avoid working at height.
12. Keep the injured as comfortable as possible. Never move the injured person unless it is essential. Utilize the first-aid kit available at the site so long the ambulance arrives.
13. It is your duty to know the location of nearest fire point from your place of work. You never know at what moment you need it. Also get yourself trained how to use different fire extinguishers.
14. Know the correct method of manual lifting. Lift correctly with legs, not by the back. If load is too heavy for a single man to lift, take help from others. Stay fit and control your weight. It is a good practice to start the job after doing some stretching exercises. It has been observed that nearly 20% of injuries occurred during lifting of materials.

15. Only the authorized drivers are allowed to drive all heavy earth moving machineries. No body other than driver should be allowed inside the driver's cabin.
16. Do not use power tools and equipments until you have been properly instructed to do so and authorized to use them.
17. Ensure that all machinery guards are in its place. Do not remove, displace, damage, or destroy any safety device provided on the machinery.
18. Do not enter inside a barricaded area.
19. If you must work around power shovels, trucks, and dozers, make sure that operators can always see you. Barricades are required for cranes.
20. Never lubricate a machine in running condition.
21. Disconnect the power source, lock out, and properly tag out the power tools before servicing, repairing or adjusting.
22. Barricade all the danger areas.
23. Excavations over1.5 m deep must be shored or sloped as required. Keep yourself out of trenches or cuts that have not been properly shored or sloped. Excavated or other materials shall not be stored nearer than 1.5 m from the edge of the excavation.
24. Use the 'four and one' rule when using a ladder, i.e., one foot of base for every four feet of height.
25. Portable ladders in use shall be equipped with safety feet unless ladder is tied, blocked or otherwise secured. Step ladders shall not be used as a straight ladder.
26. Ladders must extend three feet above landing on roof for proper use.
27. Defective ladders must be properly tagged and removed from service.
28. Keep ladder bases free of debris, hoses, wires, materials etc.

29. Build scaffolds according to the manufacturers' recommendations and construction safety standards.
30. Scaffold planks shall be properly lapped, cleated or otherwise secured to prevent shifting.
31. Use extension cords of three-prong type only. Use ground fault circuit interrupters at all times and when using tools in wet conditions; check the electrical grounding systems daily.
32. The use of safety harness in height work is essential. Use your safety lines anchored properly.
33. Never throw anything 'overboard'. Someone passing below may be seriously injured.
34. Open fires are prohibited in construction site.
35. Know what emergency procedure is established at the site you work like location of emergency phone numbers, location of first-aid kit, location of stretcher, location of fire points and evacuation plans etc.
36. Never enter a manhole, well, shaft, tunnel, or other confined space which could possibly have a non respirable atmosphere because of lack of oxygen or presence of toxic or flammable gas. Make certain a competent person tests the confined area with an appropriate detector before entry and necessary safety equipments must be worn. Stand-by persons should be stationed at the entrance.

CONSTRUCTION SAFETY ACT

1. Introduction

The construction industry is one of the oldest and most hazardous industries contributing to a high rate of fatal and serious accidents. Statutory protection has been provided to the building and construction workers through this Act.

The construction safety act is called as **"Building and other construction workers (Regulation of Employment and Conditions of Services), Act, 1996"** (No. 27 of 1996) has been passed by the parliament and received the assent of the President on 19th August, 1996. The Act is applicable with effect from 1st March 1996.

2. Objective

To regulate the employment and conditions of service of building and other construction workers and to provide for their safety, health and welfare measures and for other matters connected therewith or incidental thereto.

3. Applicability

Every establishment which employs, or had employed on any day of the preceding 12 months, 50 or more building workers in any building or other construction work.

4. Definitions

Building and other construction work:

The construction, alteration, repairs, maintenance or demolition of, or in relation to buildings, streets, roads, railways, train ways, air fields, irrigation, drainage, embankment and navigation works, flood control works, generation, transmission and distribution of power, water works, oil and gas installations, electric lines, wireless, radio, television, telephone, telegraph and overseas communications, dams, canals, reservoirs, water courses, tunnels, bridges, viaducts, aqua ducts, pipe lines, towers, cooling towers, transmission towers, etc. but does not include any building of other construction work to which the provisions of the Factories Act, 1948 or the Mines Act, 1952 apply.

Building worker:

A person who is employed to do any skilled, semiskilled, or un-skilled, manual, supervisory, technical or clerical work for hire or reward in connection with any building or other construction work but does not include a person who is employed mainly in managerial or administrative capacity, draws wages exceeding one thousand six hundred rupees per mensem or exercises, either by the nature of duties attach to the office or by reason of the powers vested in him, functions mainly of a managerial nature.

Establishment:

"Establishment" means any establishment belonging to or under control of, government, any body corporate or firm, an individual or association or other body of individuals which or who employs building workers in any building or other construction work; and includes an establishment belonging to a contractor, but does not include an individual who employs such workers in any building or construction work in relation to his own residence, the total cost of such construction not being more than rupees ten lakhs.

Employer:

In relation to an establishment, means the owner thereof, and include:

(i) In relation to a building or other construction work carried on by or under the authority of any department of the government, directly without any contractor, the authority specified in this behalf, or where no authority is specified, the head of the department.

(ii) In relation to a building or other construction work carried on by or on behalf of a local authority or other establishment, directly without any contractor, the chief executive officer of that authority or establishment.

(iii) In relation to a building or other construction work carried on by or through a contractor, or by the employment of building workers supplied by a contractor, the contractor.

Contractor:

Means a person who undertakes to produce a given result for any establishment, other than a mere supply of goods or articles of manufacture, by the employment of building workers or who supplies building workers for any work of the establishment, and includes a sub-contractor.

Appropriate Government:

Means:

- In relation to an establishment (which employs building workers either directly or through a contractor) in respect of which the appropriate Government under the Industrial Disputes Act, 1947 (14 of 1947), is the Central Government, the Central Government.
- In relation to any such establishment, being a public sector undertaking, as the central government may by notification specify which employs building workers either directly or through a contractor, the Central Government.

5. Main Provisions Relating to Safety

- **Constitution of Safety Committee:** The employer of every establishment ordinarily employing five hundred or more building workers shall constitute a safety committee of such number of representatives of the employer and equal number of the building workers.
- **Appointment of Safety Officer:** The employer of every establishment ordinarily employing five hundred or more building workers shall appoint a Safety Officer possessing a professional qualification.

- **Notice of Certain Accidents:** Employer of any establishment shall give notice of an accident which causes death or which causes bodily injury because of which the person injured is prevented from the working for a period of 48 hours or more following the accident.

  The concerned authority would make investigation if accident causes death of five or more persons. It shall make an inquiry into such accident within one month of receipt of the notice.

- **Registration of Establishment:** All Assistant Labor Commissioners (Central) have been notified as Registering Officer under the Act.

  Every establishment shall make an application to the Registering Officer for the registration of establishment within a period of 60 days from the commencement of the Act.

  The Registering Officer shall register the establishment and issue a certificate of registration to the employer.

- **Responsibility of Employer:** An employer shall be responsible for providing constant and adequate supervision of any building or other construction work in the establishment to ensure compliance with the provisions of this Act relating to safety and for taking practical steps necessary to prevent accidents.

- **Rules for the Safety and Health of Building Workers:** The appropriate Government may makes rules regarding the measures to be taken for the safety and health of the building workers in the course of their employer and the equipments and appliances necessary to be provided to them for ensuring their safety, health and protection.

Such rules may provide for all or any of the following matters:

— The safety means of access to, and the safety of, any working place, including the provision of suitable and sufficient scaffolding at and various stages when work can not be done safely from the ground or from any part of a building or from a ladder or such other means of support.

— The precautions to be taken in connection with the demolition of the whole or any substantial part of a building or other structure under the supervision of a competent person and the avoidance of the danger from collapse of any building or other structure while removing any part of the framed building or other structure by shoring or otherwise.

— The handling and use of explosive under the control of competent person so that there is no exposure to the risk of injury from explosion or from flying material.

— The erection, installation, use and maintenance of transporting equipment, such as locomotives, trucks, wagons and other vehicles and trailers and appointment of competent person to drive or operate such equipment.

— The erection, installation, use and maintenance of hoists, lifting appliances and lifting gear including periodical testing and examination and heat treatment, where necessary, precautions to be taken while raising or lowering loads, restrictions on carriage of persons and appointment of competent persons on hoists or other lifting appliances.

- The adequate and suitable lighting of every workplace and approach there to, of every place where raising or lowering operations with the use of hoists, lifting appliances or lifting gears are in progress and of all operations dangerous to building workers employed.
- The precautions to be taken to prevent inhalation of dust, fumes, gases or vapors during any grinding, cleaning, spraying or manipulation of any material and steps to be taken to secure and maintain adequate ventilation of every working place or confined space.
- The measures to be taken during stacking and un-stacking, stowing or unstowing of materials or goods or handling in connection there with.
- The safe guarding of machinery including the fencing of every fly-wheel and every moving part of a prime mover and every part of transmission or other machinery, unless it is in such a position or of such construction as to be safe to every worker working on any of the operations and as if it were securely fenced.
- The safe handling and use of plant, including tools and equipment operated by compressed air.
- The precautions to be taken in case of fire.
- The limits of weight to be lifted or moved by workers.
- The safe transport of workers to or from any workplace by water and provision of means for rescue from drowning.
- The steps to be taken to prevent danger to workers from live electric wires or apparatus includ-

ing electrical machinery and tools and from electrical wires.

- The keeping of safety nets, safety sheets and safety belts where the special nature or the circumstances of work render them necessary for the safety of the workers.
- The standards to be complied with regard to scaffolding, ladders and stairs, lifting appliances, ropes, chains and accessories, earth moving equipment and floating operational equipment.
- The precaution to be taken with regard to pile driving, concrete work, work with hot asphalt, tar or other similar things, insulation work, demolition operations, excavation, underground construction and handling materials.
- The safety policy, that is to say, a policy relating to steps to be taken to ensure the safety and health of building workers, the administrative arrangements therefore and the matter connected therewith, to be framed by the employees and contractors for the operations to be carried on in a building or other construction work.
- The information to be furnished to the Bureau of Indian Standards established under the Bureau of Indian Standards Act, 1986 (63 of 1986), regarding the use of any article or process covered under the Act in a building or other construction work.
- The provision and maintenance of medical facilities for building workers.

The Central Government may frame model rules in the matters as mentioned above. The rules in this respect are being framed and will be notified.

- **Inspecting staff**

Director General of Inspection

The Central Government has appointed the Chief Labor Commissioner (Central) as the Director General of Inspectors under the Act. He is responsible for laying down the standards of inspection and also exercise the powers of an Inspector throughout India in relation to all the establishments for which the Central Government is the appropriate government.

Chief Inspector of Inspection

The State Government may appoint Chief Inspector of Inspection of Building and Construction responsible for effectively carrying out the provisions of this Act in the State and shall also exercise powers of an Inspector throughout the state in relation to establishments for which the State Government is the appropriate Government.

Inspectors

The Government of India has appointed the following officers to be the Inspectors under the Act.

- Joint Chief Labor Commissioner (Central) New Delhi.
- All Deputy Chief Labor Commissioners (Central).
- All Regional Labor Commissioners (Central).
- All Assistant Labor Commissioners (Central).
- Chief Advisory (Labor Welfare) Office (Central), New Delhi.
- All Labor Enforcement Officers (Central).

Powers of Inspectors

(a) Enter, at all reasonable hours, with such assistants (if any) being persons in the service of the Government or any local or other public authority as he thinks fit, any premises or place where building or other construction work is carried on, for the purpose of examining any register or record or notices required to be kept or exhibited by or under this Act, and require the production thereof for inspection.

(b) Examine any person whom he finds in any such premises or place and who, he has reasonable cause to believe, is a building worker employed there in.

(c) Require any person giving out building or other construction work to any building worker, to give any information, which is in his power to give with respect to the names and addresses of the persons to, for and whom the building and other construction work is given out or received, and with respect to the payments to be made for the building and other construction work.

(d) Seize or take copies of such register, record of wages or notices or portions thereof as he may consider relevant in respect of an offence under this Act which he has reason to believe has been committed by the employer.

Other Applicable Statutes

Apart from the legislations entitled "Building and Other Construction Workers (Regulation of Employment and Conditions of Services) Act 1996." Following legislations are also applicable:

- Mines Act – 1952 – quarries, underground work.
- Motor Vehicles Act – Vehicles.
- Shops and Establishment Act – Offices.
- Contract Labor Act – Contract labor.
- Interstate Migrant Workers Act – Immigrant labor.
- Indian Explosives Act – explosives.
- Indian Electricity Act – use of Electricity.
- Workmen's Compensation Act – Compensations.

- Regulations Against Use of Child Labor.
- The Petroleum Act 1934 and Rules 1976.
- The Gas Cylinder Rules 1981.
- The Static and Mobile Pressure Vessels (Unified) Rules 1981.
- Regulation of Radiography.
- Air and Water Pollution Control Regulations.

Conclusion

Since construction industry is rapidly developing so all the rules and regulations must be known to the authorities for systematic completion of the project.

❒ ❒ ❒

Index

N

O

P

R

S

T

U

V

W

NOTES